Sue motivates you to action and success.

—**Brian Tracy**, ...preneur, president, Brian Tracy International

Sue Crum gets people into action with her wit, wisdom, and wonderful ideas. She helps people focus on what's important and inspires them to take action so that they can lead more focused and productive lives.

—**Patty Aubery**, president, The Jack Canfield Companies

Sue Crum is witty and wise and inspires us to achieve more, be more, and create more—all leading to better fulfillment and purpose.

—**Kathleen Seeley**, president, TSG, The Seeley Group Consulting, Inc.

Sue Crum's strategies have the power to change lives.

—**James Malinchak**, featured on ABC's hit TV show, *Secret Millionaire,* founder, BigMoneySpeaker.com

Sue inspires people in a witty and wise way to examine their lives and create more focus and calm.

—**Jill Lublin**, international speaker and best-selling author of three books, including *Guerrilla Publicity* (PublicityCrashCourse.com/freegift)

Sue motivates people with tips and techniques for gaining control of your life so you can be more focused and less stressed.

—**Michelle Prince**, America's Productivity Coach (MichellePrince.com)

This is more than a book. It is like having a real live coach by your side, helping you to clear clutter and reorganize your physical space and your calendar. The suggestions and solutions may look simple and practical but they are powerful. Sue shows you how small, specific actions can transform your life to more success and joy-filled tomorrows.

—**Jack Canfield**, co-creator, #1 *New York Times* best-selling book series *Chicken Soup for the Soul®,* author of *The Success Principles,* star of the hit movie *The Secret*

Sue Crum has a way of helping you see your time, your life and your value differently. Listen to her and things get better—FAST!

—**Jonathan Sprinkles**, TV personality, voted National Speaker of the Year (GetAndStayMotivated.com)

This is the **must have** book for those of us feeling stressed, overworked or just plain dissatisfied with various aspects of our lives. Sue has simple yet powerful strategies to get us into action and get things done. I know that I will recommend this great resource to my clients and audiences, and suggest that you check it out, too.

> —**Sharon Worsley**, CEO and founder of The 4 Diamond
> Leader, author of *The 4 Diamond Leader – How to Wake
> Up, Shake Up and Show Up in Business and Life*

Sue Crum inspires and motivates people to change for the better with her wit and wisdom. She is America's Leading Authority on Clearing Clutter, and her unique humor and common sense will keep you captivated throughout the entire book.

> —**Elizabeth Hagen**, speaker, author, coach
> ElizabethHagen.com

This book is packed with specific strategies to help those feeling overwhelmed and stressed. Sue Crum shows you how to look at your world, regain control, and create the future you deserve beginning now.

> —**Alex Kajitani**, California Teacher of
> the Year, author of *Owning It*

Sue has given a gift to those who have trouble setting priorities—what's wonderful is that it's a <u>menu</u>—you can start anywhere and achieve immediate satisfaction! This book is a fun, great read for anyone interested in clearing up their stuff of life.

> —**Stuart E. Gothold, EdD**, retired LA County
> superintendent of schools, clinical professor
> emeritus, University of Southern California

Sue Crum has come up with a surefire method to solve all the world's problems—well, maybe not the world's problems but certainly what is bugging most of us. I defy anyone to read through this book and not begin to see their immediate surroundings in a new light. No stress—just easy steps to better organization and a better life.

> —**Mike Krauss**, president, Total Secure Shredding, Inc.

If you've been waiting for just the right time to get organized, this is the book for you. Sue shows you how to break away from the stuff that is holding you back from being happier with more success and purpose.

> —**Dr. Kent Pollock II**, president, The Chiropractic Center

It's time to get on with the life you deserve and want. Sue will get you moving toward this dream. She is America's Leading Authority on Clearing Clutter.

As a full-time firefighter and professor, sometimes maintaining organization can be challenging. Implementing these strategies has already helped me to save time and energy, resulting in more production.

—**Darren Hall**, captain, Coronado Fire
Department, college professor

Sue's techniques and tools can help even the most stressed get better focus and productivity, along with balance in our lives. She offers specific strategies to get us focused on improving the one life we have! Her book is full of practical tips and tools for those on overload and overwhelm.

—**Wanny Hersey**, superintendent, Bullis Charter School

Special Free Gifts
from the Author

To help you achieve
more success,

Go To

2020Vision4Success.com/freegifts

Inspire and Motivate Others!
"Share This Book"

Retail $11.95
Special Quantity Discounts

5-20 Books	10%
21-99 Books	12%
100-499 Books	15%
500+ Books	Call for Quote

To Place an Order Contact:

(760) 803-1740

books@redteampress.com

Ricki —

YOU'VE GOT the POWER

Quick Tips to Create Calm, Increase Productivity and Transform Yourself

Keep creating Calm, increasing productivity & transforming!

#1 International Best-selling Author,

Sue Crum

RED Team Press

RTP

Sue Crum
_2/19_

Published by the RED team
P.O. Box 1061
Carlsbad, CA 92018
For information contact books@RedTeamPress.com

Cover design by Dawn Teagarden

Limits of Liability and Disclaimer of Warranty
The author and publisher shall not be liable for your misuse of this material. This book is strictly for informational and educational purposes.

Warning – Disclaimer
The purpose of this book is to educate and entertain. The author and/or publisher do not guarantee that anyone following these techniques, suggestions, tips, ideas, or strategies will become successful. The author and/or publisher shall have neither liability nor responsibility to anyone with respect to any loss or damage caused, or alleged to be caused, directly or indirectly by the information contained in this book.

ISBN-13: 978-0-9903150-3-2

Library of Congress Control Number: 2018940061

Printed in the United States of America
19 20 21 22 IS 5 4 3 2 1

For Robert
who has always been "the wind beneath my wings"

Contents

Section Three: July, August, September

You've ALWAYS

Had the Power,

My Dear.

You Just Had to Learn it

for Yourself."

- GLINDA, THE WIZARD OF OZ

Acknowledgments

I love the written word, always have and always will. I believe the power to communicate through writing is within all of us. But for some of us it is such a burning desire to put thought to paper that nothing can get in our way.

My life's journey began in a totally different career than the one I am in now, yet writing was certainly a part of that experience, for sure. Along the road of life there are so many to acknowledge: my parents for supporting my education, my teachers for instilling discipline and self-control, and friends, especially the members of my first writing group, Stride Writers: Joy Nordquist, Alice Brown, Anna Kelso and Karla Ogilvie. Without their support I never might have become a published author.

Special thanks for encouraging me goes to Jack Canfield, James Malinchak and Elizabeth Hagen. All three of them are speakers, entrepreneurs and published authors whom I hold in high regard.

A big thank you to my teeny, tiny family: The Darling Daughter, Melin, who is not only intelligent but beautiful as well and The Handsome, Helpful Husband, Robert, who has stood beside me every step of any wild journey I have endeavored. His support has been ongoing and unconditional. Our family has grown since my last book and I am ever so proud and pleased to have additional members now in our family.

This book is a compilation of some of my blog posts and articles I've written over the years. You, my readers, my coaching clients, and audience members, are my biggest inspiration. Your encouragement, enthusiasm, and feedback have been what has kept me on course.

I believe that all of us have within us the power to become what we have dreamed and imagined.

If you have picked up this book, the power to improve and become who you want is within these pages. You've got the Power NOW!

Preface

Welcome to "You've Got the Power" I'm so glad you stopped by to find out how to use the power you have and how to get more of it. Everything you need is within you. You have already been created with many talents and tools at your disposal. Here are a few more to add to your tool box.

As you can see from the Table of Contents I divided this book into seasons of the year: Part One-January, February, March; Part Two-April, May, June; Part Three-July, August, September, and Part Four-October, November, December.

However, regardless of the month you picked up this book, you can read the chapters in any order you would like. It makes no difference to me, nor in your learning.

Look over the Table of Contents.

See what is talking to you.

Read that article for inspiration and motivation.

I love hearing from my readers and would love to hear from you on how you applied one of the "powers" in this book and what changes occurred.

Please drop me a line at info@suecrum.com and share your success!

Who knows - your story might be in a future book!

*"To everything there is a season, and a time
to every purpose under the heaven ..."*

ECCLESIASTES *3:1*

Section One:
January, February, March

1. The Power of BEGINNINGS

Ah-hhhh! A NEW year! It lies in front of us like an empty, expansive, sandy beach or a blanket of beautiful, untouched snow.

What will this New Year be for you?

Is this the year you will: start a business, get married, change careers or jobs, move to the place of your dreams, clear up the home you are living in, meet the person you were meant to meet, write that book, complete that painting, start a family, buy or sell that business?

Whatever you are dreaming, my hope for you is that you get down on paper the specific steps to make those dreams actually come true. Take some think time by yourself to dream a little, but don't stop there. If you could only make one of those dreams happen for you, which one would it be?

What actions could you take this year that you have not done before to make that dream a reality? We all know the definition of insanity – doing the same thing over and over, but expecting a different outcome. So don't get into that.

IT'S ONLY TOO LATE IF YOU DON'T START NOW!

"You raze the old to raise the new."

– JUSTINA CHEN

"Set fire to the broken pieces; start anew."

– LAUREN DeStafano

"In a spirit of hope and new beginnings, we linked arms like a couple of kids. Pushing aside sad thoughts, we strode off into our future."

– A.B. SHEPHERD

2. The Power of CHOICE

Happy NEW Year!

Picture a clean slate, a really white-whiteboard, or a perfectly manicured lawn.

These are the images that I conjure up while contemplating the year ahead. What will it bring? Will I be different than the year before? Will the year bring more pleasure than pain? More fun than failure? More happiness than heartache?

I love new beginnings, but I'm old enough to realize that just because the calendar moved to a new year nothing about me will be new unless I choose to change and improve. If you were like me, perhaps you were waiting in great anticipation for the end of one year and the beginning of a new one.

Now we are in it. Hope you didn't make any New Year's Resolutions because the research doesn't support that these can be successful. So let those go right now - release them to the universe. Instead, let's think about change from the inside - the choices we make each and every day.

We live in a democracy and have so much control over the choices we make. As we look ahead to the vastness of the new year with all its promise, let's agree to promise ourselves that we can control so much that happens to us.

If we want more happiness, let's appreciate the people and gifts that are already in our lives.

If we want more gratitude, let's keep a Gratitude Journal and record three things each night we are grateful for or start filling a Gratitude Jar each time we have a "win," however we define win.

If we want more time in the new year, let's keep a time log for a week and see where our time goes, since all of us get the same 168 hours each week.

If we want less stuff in our lives, let's choose to release to the universe on a regular basis items that no longer make us happy and that others could use.

If we want to be healthier, let's choose one of the following to begin: keeping track of daily steps, recording food eaten in a daily food log, creating a routine with an accountability partner to meet at the gym or go for a power walk.

If we want to grow our business or start a business, we need to choose to schedule time on one's calendar to explore, interview, evaluate and decide if that is for you.

If we want to meet a partner in the new year, let go of the fact that he or she will be ringing the doorbell before Super Bowl Sunday and come up with an action plan to be out in the world where we can meet new people on a regular basis.

We don't have to declare for the new year that we are going to save the world or run for president of the United States. All of us have choices we can make moving forward, yet our small, smart choices can have enormous impact for ourselves and our families.

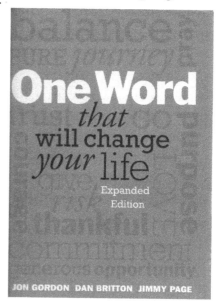

What choices can you make this month to get this new year off to Your Best Year Yet?

There is a powerful, little book that might kickstart your year. The book is "One Word That Will Change Your Life" by Gordon, Britton & Page. Instead of a list of lofty New Year's Resolutions, a lengthy list of goals, or a new mission statement for your company or organization, take a look at getoneword.com. You will be inspired to see the Power of One Word.

I have shared this approach with audiences as well as family members. One needs to sit quietly and not rush into selecting a word for the year, but rather reflect on who you are, where you are heading, and what word can serve as a compass to guide you through the rocky waters of life as well as the accolades.

Printing the word on a small rock or a 3 x 5 card to read daily can keep one inspired and serves as a foundation for everything you want to build from there. Think about making it your screen saver. My word last year was "RELEASE" and it served as my anchor through the peaks and valleys of that year.

After thought and reflection one year my word was "GIVING." A couple of family members have selected "HEALTH" and "STRENGTH." Each new year pick a new word and lean into it. Live the word for the year.

> *"There are two primary choices in life: to accept conditions as they exist, or accept the responsibility for changing them."*
>
> – DENIS WAITLEY

> *"One's philosophy is not best expressed in words; it is expressed in the choices one makes…and the choices we make are ultimately our responsibility."*
>
> – ELEANOR ROOSEVELT

> *Because almost everything - all external expectations, all pride, or fear of embarrassment or failure - these things just fall away in the face of death, leaving only what is truly important."*
>
> – STEVE JOBS

3. The Power of INTENTION

Don't have your resolutions going in one year and out the other! - Adobe Garamond Pro 12/13

If you've made New Year's Resolutions in the past and found them to be a fleeting memory by the middle of January, promise yourself that this year you won't do that. Don't go for big, giant changes for your life or lifestyle. Instead, think of small ways you can revamp or revise certain behaviors or habits.

Maybe you've been bowled over with too much football or have quickly changed the channel as soon as you've seen the sights of big men running up and down a field of snow, sleet or slippery stuff. If you have, you've missed how football serves as a metaphor for our lives.

Football games ARE very much like life. Let me explain -

For years I never understood the game of football. I thought it was a man's game, something only for boys and, well, bigger boys. In the past 20 years I've actually become a card-carrying college football season pass holder and have learned to really enjoy the game! During this time I've seen the similarities to real life through the various plays.

Often, people think about New Year's Resolutions every January. I'd rather you think of solutions, instead. In football the players have problems to solve and they have to strategize and redirect, depending on what the opposing team is doing.

Their goal is to get the ball down the field to the other end zone and score. This seems simple enough; however, the opposite team works hard to prevent that from happening.

Think about your goals for this new year - picture getting to the end zone and scoring big!

Is this the year you want to get a promotion, buy a house, start a business, find the love of your life, or clear the clutter from your environment? Whatever you are thinking for your "end zone" **score**, you need a plan - a strategy to get from here to there.

Just for this month think about your intentions. Visualize your life with clearer purpose, less stress, more balance and your priorities on straight. Now think of one small place where you could get started, and take a small step forward. What do you intend to do with this gift of over 350 days ahead?

In football what I have found fascinating is the players' ability of focus and perseverance. No one is winning games with all "Hail Mary" passes, halfway down the field.

Instead, the winners are adjusting their strategies one play at a time. Sometimes the quarterback throws the ball just a short distance; sometimes he keeps the ball himself and runs with it, and then sometimes he hands it off to someone else to run the ball. And yes, sometimes he throws the ball quite a distance (the Hail Mary Pass).

The point is that the strategy varies depending on the circumstances, but always the goal is to keep moving forward, get at least 10 yards and keep the offense on the field, even if the play only accomplishes a few yards at a time.

What small steps could you put in place this month to move forward your intentions for the new year? Forget giant "Hail Mary" passes and think small actions.

It is the winter season, but that doesn't mean we can't stay active. If where you live has very cold weather, don't just hibernate for the month. Invite friends over for an afternoon or evening of games or fellowship.

Join a book club. Plan on meeting a friend at the gym for a class. Stay connected to others.

If you're in Southern California or somewhere with mild weather, keep moving. Slap on a pedometer and get outside. Sure, we get some inclement (translation - rainy weather) this time of year, but nothing like other parts of the country.

The important part is to get moving, whatever that is for your body.

"Begin with the end in mind."

– Dr. Stephen Covey

"Our intention creates our reality."

– Dr. Wayne Dyer

"Every journey begins with the first step of articulating the intention and then becoming the intention."

– Bryant McGill

"Name your intention."

– Patti Digh

4. The Power of VISUALIZATION

*"And now let us believe in a long year that is given to us,
new, untouched, full of things that have never been."*

- RAINER MARIA RILKE

Happy New Year!   Happy New You!

What do you picture for the new year? Hopefully, you didn't make New Year's Resolutions as they tend to get broken long before Super Bowl Sunday.

Speaking of football, even if you never, ever watch football or have played the game, there are so many analogies to life with this game. As we head to the college football championship game on Monday and the Super Bowl next month, let's look at the comparisons.

Long before the players ever take the field, time is spent in the planning phase. The goal for each and every game is to win; that never changes. What changes are the steps necessary to get there. Yes, the team members visualize winning the game, but do you think they would have made it to the pro level if that is all they did?

Time is spent prior to the execution of the game on analyzing the challenges and developing an action plan, which includes specific strategies to be at their best. Once in the game they use a variety of these steps to reach their goal: short passes, long "Hail Mary" passes, the quarterback keeping the ball and running with it, or handing the ball off to someone to run with it. The great teams mix these up to confuse their opponents, as they strive to keep the ball in their possession and keep on moving. They keep their eye on the ball and their end goal, winning, in continuous focus.

So, what do you want to win at this year? Visualize it - smell it - taste it. Once we get our environments in their best shape, we open up a world of possibilities that we could not have imagined before. The new year awaits us all with a clean slate of opportunities. What will you do to win at this game of life this year?

A great way to start a new year is by creating a Vision Board. This is a most powerful tool and can be done fast and focused or slow and special - your choice. Also, it can be done in a group or alone. Your decision.

Fast and Focused: With a small bulletin board, some paper and markers, just write in block letters some things you would like to have occur by December 31 of the new year. Here are just some ideas; write your own: New Job. Graduate School. Credit Cards Paid Off. New Relationship. Storage Unit-emptied. Garage-organized. More Time Enjoying Life. Less Clutter-More Happiness. More Sunsets. A special vacation. Pin these to the board in any arrangement that you like and put the year at the top of the board. You can add pictures and words you think of during the month(s) ahead. Hang where you will see it during the year. Better yet, read it aloud each and every morning.

Really Fast: Make a wordle. Go to wordle.net and type in a group of words that represent your vision for the new year. In an instant you will have your own specialized word cloud!

Slower Yet Special: With a piece of foam board or tag board (11 x 14 or larger if you like), stack of old magazines, markers, glue, any newspaper headlines or words that speak to you, a scissors and a block of time (2 hours or so), cut out words, pictures or letters to make words of your vision for the new year. You can also get words and pictures using the internet.

Arrange and glue down on your board, putting the new year at the top, and the pictures in any arrangement you find that you like, building a collage of your vision for the year.

You now have the beginning kernels for a new year! But just as the professional athletes and Olympians know, visualization is not enough. Take each one of those ideas and analyze where you are now and what specific steps you need to make those visions a reality.

"We shape our environments and our environments shape us."

– Sir Winston Churchill

"The focus now...is on staying focused."

– Sue Crum

"A place for everything and everything in its place."

– Benjamin Franklin

5. The Power of the S.M.A.R.T. START

The new year is here already! Where did the time go? Did you get done all the things you had hoped for in the last year? Don't beat yourself up about uncompleted projects.

As Emerson said so well, "Finish each day and be done with it. You have done what you can... Tomorrow is a new day..."

Let's take the same view and change "finish each day" to "finish last year and be done with it." We now have a fresh year, a fresh start, a clean slate. View the new year as a new box of crayons. We have the ability to color it anyway we would like.

Are you one who has made New Year's Resolutions in the past? May I suggest you make NONE this year? According to the Farmer's Almanac, 88% of adults make New Year's Resolutions, yet only 20% keep them. The two most popular ones revolve around losing weight and getting organized.

There are problems with New Year's Resolutions. Often, they are made at a holiday gathering and have not been well thought out. Sometimes we've had a drink or two and come out with something so silly we have a slim chance of completing the task. By Super Bowl Sunday we barely remember what the resolutions were. No chance of success here.

This year instead of New Year's Resolutions, think "Goal-KEEPING." What do I mean? Let's commit to a small set of S.M.A.R.T. Goals with benchmark progress points along the way and build in some rewards as we meet those.

S.M.A.R.T. Goals are:

Specific

Measurable

Action-oriented

Reasonable

Timely

New Year's Resolution – "I'm going to get organized in the new year"

S.M.A.R.T. Goal – "By February 28 I am enjoying my cleared-out space in my bedroom that I've turned into a serene retreat."

Do you see the difference? One is just some nebulous idea to get organized, while the other is very specific, easily measured and reasonable to accomplish in eight weeks with some action needed.

What in your life are you ready to clear out?

-Too many things?

-Too many calendar commitments?

-Too many negative people in your world?

This year:

1. Sit down in a quiet spot. Find fifteen golden minutes. Write out an Ideal Scene for this year - how would you like the year to unfold for you; how would you like your home to feel, the people you interact with, your day to day life. Create the ideal picture and commit it to paper.

2. Next break the paragraph into parts and write a S.M.A.R.T. Goal for each area from your Ideal Scene.

3. Think of small rewards for yourself when you achieve each goal. Just like when we were youngsters, we still thrive on rewards and recognition for work done well.

4. Start with small steps, so as to build success and momentum. If this is your year to de-clutter and get organized, don't begin with tearing apart a three-car garage. Start with the car glove compartment or the trunk.

Letting go of what is no longer serving us can be very cathartic and liberating. We have to continue to ask ourselves the hard questions, "Is this item still serving me? Is it something I really need and love?

Is there anyone else who could use it more than I?"

By letting go and lightening up, we'll step lighter through the new year.

Where will you START?

"The journey of a thousand miles begins with one step."

– Lao Tsu

"Detach yourself from your stuff."

– Dr. Wayne Dyer

6. The Power of GRATITUDE

Happy Valentine's Week!

What's that you say? You didn't receive any valentines? You didn't give any valentines? I say, stop with the pity party and love where you are right now!

February is the perfect month to reflect and give thanks for whatever blessings we may have. The size of our home is not of importance; rather the love we experience there and the feeling of comfort and safety are really what matters. Some people are miserable in 5,000 square feet of living space, while others live in appreciation, happiness and calm in less than 500 feet. When we can nurture an attitude of gratitude for what we do have, we are ready to move forward and achieve more.

If you have never done any journaling, I propose doing this for the next four weeks. At the beginning or end of the day, just jot down 3-5 good things that happened that day. No fancy journal book is needed. This can be started in a small spiral notebook. The power of this is getting quiet and doing some inner reflections. Five-ten minutes of time are all that is required.

Still not sure what to do? With pen in hand, think of three-five things, people or events that you are most grateful for, and record them with the date in your notebook. Some ideas: blue sky day, great walk with a friend, reading a super book, ate just enough-not too much today, kissed my children, cleared a junk drawer, donated to my favorite charity, got a lot accomplished at work.

A gratitude journal is a superb way to begin or end each day. Once we get in the habit of doing this we will begin to be more aware of our energy shifting and feel more appreciation to how really blessed we already are, whether we received a ton of valentines or none.

I wrote about the power of vision boards earlier. Let's take your vision for the new year and pick an area of focus for our homes. When we bring calm and order to our homes, that peace carries over to all the other parts of our life, including our world at the workplace. Many people ask me where should I start; I really want to de-clutter and be organized for good this year, have more energy and be efficient, but I don't know where to begin, they ask.

A couple of thoughts: As the home is our safety net from the outside world, our bedroom is the sanctuary from the rest of the house. Ask yourself, is mine a true sanctuary, a respite of peace and calm or is at a cacophony of chaos and calamity? If you answered the latter, that is probably the place to put your focus. Spend the next few weeks bringing your bedroom back to an oasis of rest, relaxation and a place to replenish yourself. Remove items from the bedroom that really belong elsewhere. If you don't already make your bed, start that as a new habit. A made bed takes up 80% of the bedroom and looks fabulous each time you walk by, providing a sense of calm and tranquility.

If your bedroom is already peaceful, pleasant and pretty darn perfect, select a different room in your home or office to focus your attention. What hot spot exists that you've been meaning to get to, but just haven't? Here are some ideas: entryway, your car, kitchen, living/family room, desktop. Just pick one and see if you can look at the space with a "stranger's eye" and clear up any unnecessary clutter that belongs elsewhere.

Don't take on the whole world.

Just put your focus on one space, and keep your energies there.

Start to fall in love again with where you are planted!

> *"Have nothing in your houses that you do not know*
> *to be useful or believe to be beautiful."*
>
> - WILLIAM MORRIS

> *"There's no place like home."*
>
> -DOROTHY, THE WIZARD OF OZ

"I am only one, but I am one. I cannot do everything, but I can do something and I will not let what I cannot do interfere with what I can do."

- EDWARD EVERETT HALE

"At the moment of commitment, the universe conspires to assist you."

- GOETHE

"I get up every morning determined to both change the world and have one hell of a good time. Sometimes this makes planning my day difficult."

-

E.B.White, author of Charlotte's Web

7. The Power of TIME

Every four years we are granted an extra day in February. Even with this extra day we still often can't get everything done. Everyone tries to manage time, and more often than not fails. Lots of articles and people discuss time management. There are seminars one can take, books one can read, websites one can peruse, and apps to get. However, to me, it really isn't a case of time management, but rather managing ourselves better and smarter.

We all get the same amount of time each week - 168 hours. No one gets less and no one gets more. Time really is the all-time equalizer. Jerry Seinfeld once joked about saving time-saying something about "what is this thing about saving time-can we really save it up and when we get to the end of our life, use it then?"

So let's evaluate our February: Have we been busy? Have we been real busy? Or have we been productive? In the great little book, "The One Who Is Not Busy" by Darlene Cohen, she asks an all-important question that goes to the source of our busyness - "Do we actually have too much to do, or are we just approaching our work too frenetically?"

Yes, we want to be productive and lead meaningful lives, but we need to balance times of busyness with times of "not busy."

Those times of not busy allow us to dream, to think, to plan, to scheme, and just to be and breathe.

Stephen Covey and many other experts believed in the power of planning, creative thinking, goal setting and decision making. There is little visible activity with this type of work, but it can result in fabulous, concrete results and goal attainment.

So, take some quiet time as you march into March, and sit still long enough to envision clearer spaces, a more Zen environment at home or work, and getting more done with less "running around" and busyness. Just picture YOU in March-the essence of productivity with calm, clarity, and a cool head!

"I was passionate. I found something that I loved. I could be all alone in a big, old skating rink and nobody could get near me, and I didn't have to talk to anybody because of my shyness. It was great!"

- DOROTHY HAMILL, GOLD MEDAL WINNER

"Passion is energy. Feel the power that comes from focusing on what excites you."

- OPRAH

"Nothing is as important as passion. No matter what you want to do with your life, be passionate."

- JON BON JOVI

8. The Power of ENGAGEMENT

Maybe you're reading this in February and thinking, "Aahh – engagement! Isn't that sweet – getting engaged in February, the month of love and passion."

But I'm not talking about that kind of engagement. I want us to focus this month on the power of being "engaged" with the people right in front of us or the task staring us in the face. We live in such a state of distraction that sometimes it's hard to stay focused and engaged in the present.

Think about your habits and if any of them need replacing for this still "very young" new year. Have you found your brain wandering to other tasks or other people when you are with friends, family or business associates? Do you postpone tasks and assignments you know you need to accomplish and wait until the last minute to begin? Sometimes we sabotage ourselves by then saying that we didn't have enough time to do a good job, that we could have done it better if only we'd had enough time.

For this month think of one particular person or one specific task that could really use your attention and focus. When you are with that person, listen intently and stay fully engaged in their concerns, their successes and their challenges. Work to not let your eyes wander or your fingers exit to your mobile devices. Stay in the present and engage with this special person, whether that be a spouse or significant other, a family member, a friend or business colleague. Ask your brain to give 100% of your undivided attention to this special someone. Do this behavior for the remainder of the days in February, placing a check mark on your calendar each day and see if this one change does not have a positive impact on that relationship.

As Stephen Stills says, "Love the one you're with."

Now pick a specific task you have been postponing for some time and decide that February is the month you will fully engage in this. It could be a large project you have put off waiting for a giant clearance on your calendar or for the holidays to pass or the football season to end. Ask yourself what is one action step you could take on this project. It might not be the first step; it could be a middle step. The important thing is to block out at least 60-90 minutes of uninterrupted time and get fully engaged in this task.

Sometimes the hardest thing is just to start. So get started now; the year is still young and full of promise. It's only too late if we never begin!

"Live in the moment...for it is the only moment we have..."
— STEPHEN RICHARDS

"The more choices we have, the greater the need for focus."
— TOM BUTLER-BOWDON

"The only way to do great work is to love what you do."
— STEVE JOBS

"You can make more friends in two months by being interested in other people than you can in two years by trying to get people interested in you."
— DALE CARNEGIE

9. The Power of ACTION

"The secret of getting ahead is getting started. The secret of getting started is breaking your complex overwhelming tasks into small manageable tasks, and then starting on the first one."

– MARK TWAIN

Rather than New Year's Resolutions which become buried under the guacamole and chips by Super Bowl Sunday, the One Word Challenge has the potential to have a lot more meat on its bones.

New Year's Resolutions tend to be so general and made "off the cuff" that they rarely have a chance to survive, let alone get "resolved."

Each new year always offers us an opportunity for new growth, new change and new beginnings. For many of us one year rolls into the next and with a blink of an eye it seems that years have just disappeared like rolling waves.

You may be skeptical about how One Word can change or improve your year. What the One Word does is give you a focus, a direction for the year ahead. Here are some examples:

- transform
- commitment
- well-being
- possibility
- triumph
- expansion
- balance
- focus
- change

So let's build on that. Many people begin the new year doing either New Year's Resolutions or Vision Boards or both. I'm here to tell you none of that, including having a One Word, will work to bring about improvement or change!

What WILL make a difference is Taking ACTION!

What holds us back sometimes is Fear…fear of failure, fear of the unknown, fear of not knowing all the right steps, and even fear of success. What fear really stands for is:

+ **F**alse
+ **E**xpectations
+ **A**ppearing
+ **R**eal

Our mind plays tricks on us and freezes our ability to move forward.

So…what ACTIONS will you take this year? Start a business? Write a book? Clear your clutter? Meet your soul-mate? Move to a home just the right-size for you? Become a parent? A grandparent? Make amends with a loved one? Pay back taxes? Or _____?

We don't have to have the whole road map in front of us. When we start on any journey, we don't have to know every turn on the highway. As we progress, we get feedback telling us whether or not we are on the right road.

Action steps are just like that. In order to get feedback we have to step forward.

So step into the new year with conviction, commitment and continuous effort!

> *"Life is like riding a bicycle. In order to keep*
> *your balance you must keep moving."*
> -ALBERT EINSTEIN

10. The Power of the LEAP

About every four years we are gifted with an extra day in February, February 29. This extra day was added many centuries ago as a corrective measure for the calendar. We've probably all heard some of the traditions and superstitions about this date, the one most popular being that women could propose to men either on February 29 or during Leap Month or even any time during a Leap Year.

As you are reading this, pretend it's Leap Year and decide to set a really big goal for yourself for the new year. My mentor and friend, Jack Canfield, calls these BHAGs. A BHAG is defined as a Big Hairy Audacious Goal. While Jack also teaches making S.M.A.R.T. goals each year in the various aspects of one's life, like financial, health, and relationships, he does promote setting at least one BHAG that will really stretch a person and can catapult them to new heights.

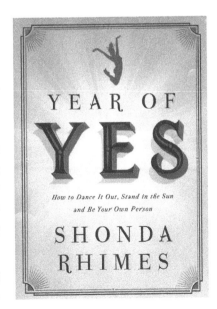

What could LEAP you way forward in your life? a new career? starting a business? finding a soulmate? moving to a home that is the right-size for you? getting out of paying rent for storage units? changing jobs? writing that book? decluttering and organizing your life and stuff?

I've recently started reading "Year of Yes" by Shonda Rimes.

Her name may sound familiar to you. She is the writer and creator of several hit TV shows, including "Grey's Anatomy", "SCANDAL", and "How to Get Away with Murder." In 2014 she decided to make that year her Year of Yes, after one of her sisters told her "you never say yes to anything." It became Shonda's challenge for the new year, pondering how many uncomfortable opportunities could she say yes to doing.

The book reports out her experiences and reflections on that year.

In other words, Shonda took a Big LEAP!

What BHAG or LEAP would you like to take for this year?

"Everything you want is on the other side of fear."

- JACK CANFIELD

"I advise you to say your dream is possible and then overcome all inconvenience, ignore all the hassles and take a running leap through the hoop, even if it is in flames."

- LES BROWN

"Take a leap of faith and begin this wondrous new year by believing. Believe in yourself. And believe that there is a loving Source - a Sower of Dreams-just waiting to be asked to help make your dreams come true."

- SARAH BAN BREATHNACH

"You don't have to get it perfect; you just have to get it going. Babies don't walk the first time they try, but eventually they get it right."

- JACK CANFIELD

11. The Power of PAPER

Yikes! It's March already!

We are heading to the end of the first quarter of the year and with that looming deadline there's one right behind it –

Which deadline is that, you ask?   April 15!

As we've all heard there are two things we can count on in this world: death and taxes!

Leaving death alone for now, we are right smack in the middle of tax season.

Does this year have you MAD again at yourself that you are MARCHING through your home or office looking for all those important papers from last year?

If so, now is the time to grab hold and say – no more!

Paper management continues to be a problem for most people. While a paperless society has been discussed since the 1970s, many of us are still drowning in it. If that is you, here are a few quick steps to get you marching through the mayhem without all the madness!

If your papers are everywhere:

Grab at least six banker's boxes. These are available at any office supply store. They are easy to assemble, come with lids, and are made of cardboard and very inexpensive. If you have papers in every room, you will need more than six boxes.

When we are drowning, what do we need? We need to build …
R A F T S!

Label the first five boxes R (for reading material), A (for action items-you need to do something with this- pay a bill, call someone, give to tax person, etc.), F (for file-you have taken action but now just want to file for reference), T (for toss or recycle), and S (for shred).

Line up these five boxes in the room with the most papers. Can you see the word RAFTS?

If so, you are ready to begin, once you put on your favorite dancing music and set a timer.

Start with 30-45 minutes of time. Grab a stack of paper and get sorting!

Do not stop to read the magazines or catalogs or long articles you haven't had time to read yet. Simply quickly drop then in the R box for reading.

Do not stop to complete any action item. Just drop it in the A box for action later.

Keep working and stay focused. When the timer goes off after a block of time, take a five minute break, and begin again.

Continue this with the papers you have. The time this will take you will depend on three things: 1.) the volume of loose papers you have, 2) your energy level and 3) the amount of time you schedule for this.

When papers are sorted into these five categories, place the R box by a comfortable reading chair; put the T box out for trash/recycling; put the F box in the room with your filing cabinet. If your S box of shredding is not full, set aside to keep adding to it later.

Now you are left with the A box only. On the same day or another day that you put on your schedule (depending on your energy level), go back through the A box, and remove any paper item tied to taxes for this year: W-9s, 1099s, stock transactions, business receipts, charitable contributions. Put all those in the sixth box and label it Tax Papers, and then write the year.

Hooray! Congratulate yourself that you have marched through the madness and now schedule the time to meet that April 15th deadline!

> *"Death, taxes and childbirth! There's never any*
> *convenient time for any of them."*
>
> – MARGARET MITCHELL, AUTHOR, GONE WITH THE WIND

12. The Power of HABIT

Since the start of the year, I talked about "the power of intention" in January and "the power of engagement" in February. The year is just beginning and there is time for long-lasting change when one creates the right focus.

Take a few moments and visualize your intentions for the next 12 months. Write them down as specifically as possible and make sure that you are passionate about making them a reality this year.

Now let's focus on our habits.

"We are what we repeatedly do.
Excellence then, is not an act, but a habit."

– ARISTOTLE

Everyone's situation is unique. Are there some habits you want to put in place to make yourself more efficient and productive in this year? Are some of these ones you've said year after year you were going to do, but somehow never got around to them?

When we set grandiose goals, such as lose 30 pounds, get rid of storage unit(s), or move to a home that better suits us right now, we never take the time to put in place some small, strategic steps that could aid in the accomplishment of these long-term goals. Then year after year they lose their stamina for success because we haven't created any lasting habits that could help us along the way.

Just like many of you have heard me say in the past - start small for...

BIG change!

If some of your projects are too big and you don't know where to start, think of one small step you could put in place and make into a new habit.

Want to lose weight? Get a pedometer and wear it daily.

Want your bedroom more like a sanctuary? Remove items that belong elsewhere.

Want your kitchen more tidy daily? Clean the sink nightly until it shines and clear the kitchen of any dirty dishes.

Want a calmer start to each day? Plan specifics the night before.

Build in simple routines to make your environment and life more focused and controlled. Put habits into your daily routine and build that muscle memory.

"Successful people are simply those with successful habits."

- BRIAN TRACY

"Motivation is what gets you started. Habit is what keeps you going."

- JIM ROHN

"Lead an intentional life."

- DR. LAURA SCHLESSINGER

13. The Power of MARCHING UP YOUR MOUNTAINS

Often in February, our rains in Southern California make our mountains look gorgeous-picture postcard pretty! From afar the snow often seems like whipped cream sitting atop our favorite sundaes. Up close the mountains look awesome and inspiring...

unless we are thinking of climbing them.

Then, those same big beauties look daunting and insurmountable.

Sometimes our projects and tasks look the same way. The end is so far removed from where we are standing that we can't figure out how we will ever complete them, and do a successful job as well.

Start with small steps of action. That can build the success and momentum we need. If we don't think about the entire project (or mountain) in one big gulp, but rather ask ourselves, "What's the next action that will move this forward?" That one question can keep us on track and build forward motion.

Recently I was on a ski trip at Mammoth Mountain, California where I observed disabled athletes getting around the mountain. I don't mean figuring out how to go through the food line in the lodge. I mean getting on and off the chair lifts, skiing down the slopes, and getting up when they tumbled.

This particular group is called The Achievers-how's that for a great name! On this specific weekend the members were from Orange County, California and their truck was emblazoned with the slogan "If I can do this, I can do anything."

Some of these individuals were skiing with one leg, or blind or ski-sitting in a device called a scarver. They approached each run, each turn and each challenge with confidence and eagerness. These mountains presented no fear to these very capable individuals.

Let's develop their attitude for the mountains in our lives.

What has YOU on OVERWHELM?

Is it mental clutter chatting at you?

Is it physical clutter ?

Is it people you've been seeing or places you've been going that no longer bring you joy?

Visualize that physical or emotional space totally cleared and opened up for new possibilities for you.

How would you feel?

-Lighter with your step?

-Younger with your stride?

-Healthier with your life?

Start with what is bothering you the most. Is it not enough personal time to do the things you'd like? If so, analyze your calendar and start chopping. Remove anything you absolutely can. Delegate tasks to others or hire someone who could do some of these. Perhaps a friend has a high school or college student who would like to earn some money. Defer if you can some projects that absolutely do not have to happen right now.

If it's too much physical clutter, ask yourself which area is bugging you the most. Is it the front entry? Is it the master bedroom which has become the family dumping ground? Is it the home office? Is it the walk-in closet that you can't walk in anymore? Is it space at work?

Whichever space is gnawing at you the most, that's where you should focus your energy. Where are your biggest mountains that are holding you back from leading a happy, healthy, productive life?

If the disabled athletes can face their mountains, I know you can, too, and with just as much success!

Start stepping…

"It is not enough to stare up the steps. We must step up the stairs."

– VANCE HAVNER

14. The Power of MOVEMENT

Are you marching toward your BEST YEAR YET? We are still in the first quarter of the year so there is plenty of time to "right the boat" and start steering in the direction of your dreams! But I'm not talking about movement or busyness just for the sake of activity. I'm talking about creating a clear direction and pathway for the rest of the year.

Look around at your work and home environments. Are they clogged up with projects not completed, files not put away, or just plain too much stuff? Now is a perfect time to address that stuff (or clutter) and either assign a home for the items or release them to the universe. By taking action and moving toward spaces with more breathing room, it will be much easier for you to focus and concentrate on the important, and let go of what's not important.

Change up the energy in your world of work or home and let's all get

MOO-ving this March!

M – Make a plan.

O – Out with the old, the tired, and the expired.

O – Organize the keepers and assign them specific homes where they can live!

If your home is in tip-top shape, take a look at your office space. If your office is a calm, peaceful place of productivity, look at your home environment.

No time to do this, you say?

Set a timer for 30 minutes of uninterrupted time and see what you can find in your environments that you are no longer using or need.

What could you release to the universe (by donating) so that others could benefit from things you aren't using?

Put on some dancing music – and Get MOO-ving!

It's TIME to get out of our cars, off our couches and get MOVING toward wide-open spaces and plenty of breathing room!

Let's strive for breathing space and room to line dance through life.

How can you get MOO-ving this month for fun or with family and friends?

As many of you know I love to ski and have been doing such since I left cold, flat Illinois for sunny Southern California many moons ago! The irony is not lost on me about becoming a downhill skier AFTER running away from the ice, the freezing and the wild winds of Chicago!

I followed sorority sister Sue to Southern California, and when she told me the first thing I had to do was get up on the mountains and learn to ski, I almost turned around and drove back the 2,015 miles! But…I didn't.

Over the years I actually learned how to ski and found such beauty and peacefulness in the mountains. Last month my handsome and helpful husband and I went to the site of the 2010 Olympics – Whistler, Canada, – for a ski trip. When I saw the cool sign that read "CAN-SKI" I thought, that's me! I feel blessed to keep skiing and doing something so enjoyable and with family!

What can YOU do this month to get Moving?

A walk around the block, a bike ride, jogging in the park, taking a Yoga class, swimming laps at the gym, attending Zumba, going for a hike, racquetball, signing up and training for a half-marathon, scheduling time for an exercise DVD a couple of times a week, OR putting on dancing music and moo-ving your piles out for more smiles?

Whatever you can do to move will give you more energy to make MARCH MARVELOUS!

"Take action! An inch of movement will bring you closer to your goals than a mile of intention."

— STEVE MARABOLI

"In the process of letting go you will lose many things from the past, but you will find yourself."

— DEEPAK CHOPRA

"Don't dwell on what went wrong. Instead, focus on what to do next. Spend your energy moving forward together towards an answer."

— DENIS WAITLEY

"There is no standing still because time is moving forward."

— GREG LAKE

"Every day do at least one thing that scares you."

- ELEANOR ROOSEVELT AND SUE CRUM

15. The Power of TAKING BACK CONTROL

Remember when everyone said we'd soon be living in a paperless society? Right on, you say! Believe it or not, going paperless was first discussed back in the 1970s. Since then, the topic keeps reappearing and while some have made a little headway in this department, many of us have not.

In fact, a lot of us are drowning in paper - now more than ever.

How could this be?

Think how different life is today compared to way back in the last century. Everyone now has a computer in the home and a printer. Years ago if we needed something printed we planned a trip to a store called Kinko's to handle such a task. There weren't office supply or big box stores with cases of reams and reams of copy paper. Businesses and schools ordered those kinds of products, not regular households.

In the mid 20th century folks had one catalog in their homes— Sears, Roebuck & Company. They didn't find themselves on a list receiving 10-20 catalogs every month like many homes today. We are becoming buried in our own stuff!

Those are just a couple of differences.

So what can we do about this avalanche of paper in our world?

THREE SIMPLE STEPS:

STOP

LOOK

LISTEN

STOP the flow of so much coming into your life. Remove your name from the catalog mailings, donation requests, and direct marketing campaigns of all the companies chasing you to spend your money on them. Go to worldprivacyforum.org and click on Top Ten Opt Out List.

Get your name off of as many lists as possible. In some cases you may have to do this more than once as your info could have been sold earlier to additional organizations.

DON"T bring the junk mail IN the house. Have a sorting system established right at your home's entry. Before placing in the recycle bin, be sure and remove your name or shred any individual info about you. Some people use a large black marker, while others have a shredder placed nearby. You'll be amazed how you can make the size of your incoming mail much smaller by taking this step.

LOOK at your landing pad for the incoming mail. Is it any horizontal surface?

For some folks mail lands on kitchen counters. Others in the family may put it on the stairs or lay it on the first clear space they can find. All of these behaviors have disaster written all over them.

When important bills and notices get misplaced, deadlines get missed and late fees get added!

Oh, the stress of it all!

Decide on ONE landing pad for incoming mail. If everyone in the family can't remember to use it, remove those individuals from bringing in the mail.

If yours is a busy household with many individuals, including children, set up a command center to handle important papers coming from school and backpacks. A command center can be a portable file box. Inside, each family member has a file plus other action files, such as To Pay, To Call, To Schedule, To Email, etc. You make this as specific to the actions that are important in your life.

LISTEN to your inner voice. What's causing the most havoc? Are there no assigned places for the magazines that come in or the catalogs you want to keep? Do papers from school or books get scattered all over the place? Sit quietly with a small notebook and think about where is a good home for each of those items.

Like Dorothy always said, "There's No Place Like Home."

For example, the magazines in your house need a place to be kept - a magazine rack or basket. Decide how many back issues you really need to store and think through WHEN you are going to read them.

Libraries love people who donate back issues.

If you're going to read them, decide when and where. Then move the magazine basket there and make a date with yourself for some reading time.

If your mail, magazines, and paper mayhem don't have specific homes, any home (or counter) will do and this will keep you in perilous paper pile-up!

Wishing you clear counters, lovely landing pads, and marvelous magazine moments!

> *"You leave old habits behind by starting out with the thought, 'I release the need for this in my life.'"*
>
> – Dr. Wayne Dryer

Section Two:
April, May, June

16. The Power of SPRINGTIME

Are you loving the longer days, the great sunshine and being outdoors just a little bit longer each day? Spring has sprung and with it a lot of new opportunities for us all. Along with new baby birds and flowers blooming what are some new things you want to put into your world this spring?

Perhaps it's some new habits. Let's look at how easy this can be.

If the dark afternoons and early sunsets had you inside most evenings in the winter months, think about using the longer days to get to some of those projects you've been putting off for some other time. Make this month that "some other time" and set about tackling one of those tasks in the next 30 days.

Years ago and often still in farming communities folks had big spring cleaning events, where all the coverings came off the windows and the furniture, and everything got washed until it was looking almost new. Perhaps that's a project you want to take on this spring, before summer and house guests arrive.

However, I was thinking more of our stuff- you know, the stuff that gets forgotten in the back of the cupboards or the closets-the stuff that gets darn right lonely because we never seem to use it or take it out for an outing or two.

Springtime is the perfect time to look at what we've accumulated and what we really are not using anymore. Look around your home. Is there a place where you could create some additional breathing space? Perhaps it's a closet or a cupboard. Maybe it's a pantry or a garage. How about a storage unit you've been paying rent on for years? Could you make this the last spring of doing that?

It can be as small as a junk drawer that's gotten too "junky" because of some bad habits. Think about scheduling some time in your calendar/planner and following through on your date to "just do it." If it's a small project, just keep focused on it with scheduled breaks and a big reward at the end.

If you would really like to SPRING into massive action, think about who could help you. Visualize what kind of help you need; look ahead at your calendar and select a date when you would like it finished. Get a clear visual of the new open space or the emptied garage or storage unit. Schedule this onto your calendar.

Now take some deep breaths and face the possibilities of a perfect summer with a lighter load.

"A man is the sum of his actions, of what he can do. Nothing else."
— JOHN GALSWORTHY

17. The Power of RELEASING

I hope your March Madness included some great Moo-ving! Remember we talked about:

M - Make a plan

O - Out with the old, the tired and the expired

O - Organize the keepers and assign them specific homes where they can live

I saw this life-size cow mid-March looking over the furnishings in a furniture store and thought, "She's helping everyone to get moo-ving!"

Of course, we don't need to get rid of our furniture and head out to a retail store to replace it. Sometimes less is more, and we need to focus on letting go of what's not working first.

In my book, "Clear Your Clutter: 50 Ways to Organize Your Life, Home or Business So You Can Become More Calm, Focused & Happy" I have a chapter called, "The Best Date Night of the Week (Even if You're Married)."

So many people tell me that's one of their favorite chapters in the book and always puts a smile on their face when they read it.

The steps are really quite simple, and if you are interested in releasing some clutter and stuff from an over-packed life, home or office, here is a great place to start.

Get out your calendar and note the day of the week "the trash man cometh."

Now put a big red circle on the NIGHT BEFORE. That's the BEST DATE NIGHT because it is your golden opportunity (your golden ticket) to see how many "gifts" you can have ready for the trash man before his arrival!

Put on your favorite dancing music - no need to get dressed up fancy for this date!

Grab some large hefty bags or garbage barrels and look around your environment. Is there some clutter that is no longer serving you, but taking up valuable breathing space in your home or office?

Have the recycle bins at the ready. What can you release to recycling to bring down the volume of stuff screaming at you?

Confidential papers? Get a bankers box going and mark it: "shred." When it's full, bring to a drop-off shred place of your choice.

Take a look at your spaces and places and especially the rooms you do not enjoy going into. The reason may be that you get too stressed out looking at all the stuff in that room.

Now look at those spaces with a calm, critical eye and see what you could release that is no longer serving the life you are living today.

What to do with items too big for the best date of the week? Call your favorite charity for a donation pick-up and breathe deeply knowing that you are releasing to the universe items that you've enjoyed but now others can use.

"It's not the daily increase but daily decrease. Hack away at the unessential."

\- Bruce Lee

"Some of us think holding on makes us strong, but sometimes it is letting go."

\- Herman Hesse

18. The Power of CPM - CONTINUOUS PRODUCTIVE MOVEMENT

Sometimes we wish we could wave a magic wand and life would be easier or different or more fun or even just a little bit perfect. We think with a New Year we can become a "New Me." Somehow we think that with the change of the calendar and the clock, that each new year will be different and somehow better...

all by itself.

The first quarter of the year is behind us now. It's still early in the year to create the life and environments we so imagine and deserve. Perhaps we've already tried the magic wand thing and the vision board thing and yet we still feel stuck in a rut.

Time to dust ourselves off and get serious with this one life we have! Time to "spring into action" creating our work and home environments for better health, balance and productivity. It's time to take back control so we can reduce anxiety, possess the things that bring us joy and happiness, and release to the universe what no longer serves us, thus creating breathing space for us!

Last month I suggested folks look at their master bedroom and see if it is the sanctuary from the outside world (and the rest of your home) or if it was filled with chaos and clutter. Spring is such a perfect time to examine the clothes in our closets and dressers.

Which items do we really love to wear that make us feel good and on top of the world? Our spirits soar when we wear these.

Colleagues and friends ask if we've lost weight or comment how terrific we seem because we are exuding confidence. These are the keepers.

As our seasons change it's the perfect time to look at our winter wardrobe and decide how much we really love certain outfits. Did we wear them this past winter and if not, why not?

Even for many of my working readers I suggest starting here. Beginning with your wardrobe will start the solution to taking back control of your life.

Begin with the closet, surveying the items you never wear and get a Donate bag going. Schedule time to address this and give yourself a deadline.

Keep clearing clutter.

Keep the winners and the definite "keepers."

Release to the universe what no longer serves you or that you no longer love!

Walt Disney said it so well: "The way to get started is to quit talking and begin doing."

Make time NOW to **spring into action** with fun, family and friends this summer!

What if you decided to focus the **next 60 days** on clearing clutter and creating breathing space in your home and office?

PICTURE how you want those spaces to look. VISUALIZE your happiness and productivity soaring.

IMAGINE having people stop by your desk at work and you not being embarrassed you couldn't locate an important paper.

SEE yourself having friends over this summer or not panicking when relatives and friends from afar contact you about coming to visit.

"Every day and in every way, I am becoming better and better."
– EMILE COUE

"Don't let any situation intimidate you anymore;
don't accept defeat anymore."
– JAACHYNMA N. E. AGU

"If you want a new tomorrow, then make new choices today."
– TIM FARGO

"As you improve yourself, those around you benefit and are, themselves, improved."

– BRUCE VAN HORN

"We cannot become what we want to be by remaining what we are."

– UNKNOWN

19. The Power of the SPRING FLING!

I love spring…and then I don't.

I love it because it always creates an opportunity for the new, the shedding of the old, and the imagining the impossible!

I don't love it because it signals it's a long way until next winter! If you've been reading these stories from the beginning you know I left the blizzards of Chicago many years ago, only to become a black diamond downhill skier with a season pass, here out west!

Go figure!

But back to spring. It IS a time of rebirth, redo, and reinvent. Whether it's our home environment, our work place, our calendar or our mind, spring connotes a fresh start - a new beginning. It gives us a sign of hope and new possibility.

So what could you Spring Fling for the next four weeks?

Is it time to throw open the curtains, pull back the heavy bed coverings, and take off your rose-colored glasses and really, really look at your environments?

Hopefully, by the time you are reading this, your tax returns have all been filed and you can put aside that project and begin to look forward to the spectacular summer, just months ahead.

When I am coaching clients, I help them to see their spaces through the eyes of a stranger.

Ask yourself, how long has it been since you:

put fresh new towels in your bathroom?

evaluated the number of products inside your shower?

cleared your kitchen counter tops and only put back the items you use on a regular basis?

seriously viewed your calendar obligations and created some open, breathing space?

decided to let IT go, whatever the IT is for you, and let someone else use items you are not using and/or don't absolutely LOVE by donating them to your favorite charity?

Let springtime be the time you reflect on these questions.

If you do your SPRING FLING now, you will be ready for summer in no time, enjoying the simpler speed of summer with care-freeness, calm, and contentment!

"Keep IT Moving!"

- SUE CRUM

"Get rid of clutter and you may just find it was blocking the door you've been looking for…"

-KATRINA MAYER

"Do something today that your future self will thank you for."

- UNKNOWN

20. The Power of MORE SPRING FLING

I know what you're saying...

Gee whiz, she wrote about the Spring Fling already.

Here's the thing -

Even professional organizers have stuff, and yes - do I dare say it...

CLUTTER!

For those of you who have heard me speak and have a Quote Card of mine, you know that one of my favorite quotes is

"The Best Date Night of the Week is the Night Before the Trash Man Cometh!"

When is your Best Date Night? (Fill in the blank)_____

Mine is Sunday.

So last Sunday was my day to see how many "gifts" I could get for my Marvelous Monday Man of Trash! (And recycling)

I knew exactly where I wanted to focus my energies - the garage!

Normally, my car fits nicely in the garage but ever since The Darling Daughter and The Super Son-in-law moved back to town from downtown there has been a "clutter creep" going on in there.

It started innocently enough with their move last fall, but it quickly moved out of control.

Can anyone relate here?

Their remodel wasn't finished in time for their October move-in date, so our garage was one of the stopping points for the movers. Then The Gracious Granddaughter made her appearance into the world early October instead of end of October!

Between baby gifts being sent here to garage sale items from their downtown abode to an ever-present addition and subtraction of various and sundry items they "weren't quite sure about" I had to relinquish all control of the space.

Now since spring has sprung, their year-long remodel project is, dare I say it, almost finished! This past weekend the hard-working, Super Son-in-law removed the last of the items that came out of their garage and got added to our garage while their built-in shelving was being installed.

And that was my opening!

I worked all afternoon and...

I loved it!

Clearing space.

Creating breathing room.

Finding things I had not seen in awhile.

And getting gifts for the Terrific Trash Man!

My large recycling bin for Monday pickup got filled in short order.

My car got filled with items to donate for Goodwill drop-off.

My heart got filled with happiness!

I'm almost there - I can actually visualize my car in the garage well before Mother's Day!

There's just three small boxes/bins left for them to remove.

That will be the best Mother's Day gift I can give myself!

Sometimes we have to plan on our OWN gifts to keep joy and happiness streaming into our lives!

"The best things in life aren't things"
- UNKNOWN

"Clutter is symptomatic of delayed decisions."
- CYNTHIA KYRIAZIS

21. The Power to DISCONNECT (+RECONNECT)

We are in love with our tech toys.

In so many ways they do make our lives easier. We can communicate with people far and wide, making the world seem like a much smaller space. We are able to make much magic with our mobile devices in ways our parents and grandparents never could have imagined.

Whether it be our laptops, desktops, or hand-held devices, we love them so. Who could have imagined that something that fits in the palm of our hands could be an alarm clock, a calculator, a map, a newspaper, a book, a Rolodex, a boarding pass, a camera, and so much more?

And yet, these mobile marvels are seductive and addictive. We are sure the next text, voicemail or email is so important we convince ourselves of the need to be connected to the outside world 24/7. According to many scientists we are actually getting a dopamine rush from receiving texts.

We are checking our phones 150 times a day, often watching multiple screens, according to the 2013 Kleiner Perkins Caufield & Byers Internet Trends Report. In one study by OMD UK, a London-based media agency, that asked 200 people to record how many times they go between their laptops, mobile phones and such, it was 21 times an hour, switching between tech devices.

For students, Dr. Larry Rosen, psychology professor at Cal State-Dominguez Hills, found in his research that students focused on schoolwork for about three minutes before going over to a digital distraction. He believes for those with limited time to study, students are staying up later and not functioning as well because of stress.

Everyone today boasts about how busy they are, how they are suffering from overwhelm and overload. Make the month of May a time to sit back and look at the amount of digital distractions in your life. And yes, that can be a kind of clutter for many.

When our heads are buried in our screens, what message is that giving to those around us, especially our children and grandchildren?

Is it possible to pick one day a week for a tech time-out? Some CEOs are setting the example for this, like Dan Rollman, of RecordSetter.com. He's come up with a Sabbath Manifesto that includes a day of avoiding technology and commerce, giving back and getting outside.

Now there's a great thought - getting outside.

If you feel you can't let go for a day, how about a couple of hours?

Across the country it's the perfect time of year to get into nature or to take a hike, a picnic, a walk around the block, or read a book in the yard. Let the senses kick in and really listen to the birds sing, your own deep breaths or the conversations of those you are with that day.

By disconnecting from these digital distractions, we'll be able to finish projects we've started or connect on a deeper level with those in our presence rather than those so far away.

Afraid your phone will take over and grab your focus? Tell yourself you are in charge of your life and take back control. If you think that won't work, put your phone under your pillow or in the console of your car, and be free to be you for an afternoon or a day.

"Our presence with another can be the greatest present."

– SUE CRUM

"Love the one you're with."

– STEPHEN STILLS

"Successful people maintain a positive focus in life no matter what is going on around them. They stay focused on their past successes rather than their past failures, and on the next action steps they need to take to get them closer to the fulfillment of their goals rather than all the other distractions that life presents to them."

– JACK CANFIELD

22. The Power of HAPPINESS

Keep Flinging for More Breathing Space!

Earlier I wrote about making time for a Spring Fling! Springtime is definitely the time to look at the abundance of all that we have and ask ourselves, "Do I need all of this stuff?"

For some of us we have gotten in the habit of retail therapy, thinking more will make us happier. However, after we get the items home (or they arrive in the mail) we find they are not bringing us the bliss we were expecting. Maybe we bought the items on a whim or during a late night infomercial or while we were strolling on the internet because we were either bored or were procrastinating what we knew should get done.

How do we find more happiness?

I suggest you grab some hefty bags, put on some of your favorite dance music and go through your home, room by room. Are there some things that no longer serve you, fit you, or bring you joy? Are these items clogging up your space and creating stress for you because you're not using them, they need some repair, or they were a mistake to bring home in the first place? Might someone else get some happiness from these things?

Could you grab at least 31 items for donate in the next 31 days?

Decide now when you could do this. Put that on your calendar/planner. Have your bags and music ready. When your appointment with yourself arrives, set a timer and see how quickly you can gather 31 items to donate this month.

When your bags fill up, call your favorite charity, and tell them what you have. Then schedule a pick-up. This is a great habit to get into doing.

Marci Shimoff wrote about The Myth of More in her book, "Happy for No Reason." She talks about how people think the more they have, the better they'll feel. The following statistics that she gives contradict that viewpoint:

Once personal wealth exceeds $12,000 a year, more money produces virtually no increase in happiness.

Americans' personal income has increased more than two and half times over the past fifty years, but their happiness level has remained the same.

Make May the month to lighten your load, giving you buoyancy and joy!

"How old would you be if you didn't know how old you are?"

I love this quote! I even have it in a small magnet in a tiny corner on the side of my refrigerator, so I can read it when fixing meals.

Sometimes we are so busy with our grown-up lives that we forget the simple pleasures of our childhood, the things we enjoyed doing that didn't cost much, if anything, yet brought such happiness to our lives.

Make May the month to remember those happy moments and put some of them back into your life. The following are from a sweet little book, John Hadamuscin's, *Simple Pleasures*:

Lemonade on the lawn

The smell of tea roses in bloom

Riding a bicycle

Lending a hand to a friend

Watching a butterfly dance through the garden

Taking your shoes off

A bunch of daisies on the kitchen table

A picnic in the park

Add to this list your favorite simple pleasures, and create an abundance of happiness and gratitude this month!

"Enjoy Now."

– GRETCHEN RUBIN, AUTHOR, THE HAPPINESS PROJECT

23. The Power of CLEARING

Spring has Sprung!

With spring we have the opportunity to add a "spring to our step" and get outdoors more often. The weather is picture perfect this time of year, and we have an opportunity to spend more of it in nature, whether that be at the beach, in the mountains, or just outside.

There's an energy in the air in springtime. It's an ideal time of year to face our environments, both at work and home, and ask ourselves, "Can I create more breathing space here by clearing?"

By clearing I mean really examining the items you've held on to for a long time. If everywhere you turn you see clutter, that clutter or stuff is sucking energy (the life) out of you. If you have pockets and piles of stuff in certain rooms, those are probably the rooms or places you avoid.

Even professional organizing coaches have pockets of stuff and piles. I call these "Hot Spots." Maybe not all of the organizers have this, but I can admit to you that I do. Springtime is the ideal time to address these "hot spots."

If you've heard me speak you know I believe in starting out small, rather than going big. So where can you clear this month and lighten the load you are carrying?

As for me, I'm heading to the big dark hole under my bathroom sink. It's not too big that this will be a forever spring project. All I need to do is schedule a block of time on my calendar and keep that appointment with myself.

How about you?

Is there a "hot spot" you know you could attack and clear that's been gnawing at you?

There is so much power in clearing.

Our stuff does not need to own us.

Take back control - one clearing project at a time, and see how much lighter you step into the sunshine.

"Don't let the perfect be the enemy of the good. Lower the bar. Actually spending ten minutes clearing off one shelf is better than fantasizing about spending a weekend cleaning out the basement*."

– GRETCHEN RUBIN (*SOUTHERN CALIFORNIANS – SUBSTITUTE GARAGE FOR BASEMENT ABOVE.)

"A simple life is not seeing how little we can get by with – that's poverty – but how efficiently we can put first things first... When you're clear about purpose and your priorities, you can painlessly discard whatever does not support these, whether it's clutter in your cabinets or commitments on your calendar."

– VICTORIA MORAN

24. The Power of MOMENTUM

Jump for Joy – it's June!

For many of us June brings up memories of summers past or the possibilities of making this summer super special.

June is like a blank whiteboard, just waiting to be filled in with delicious delights.

But before we go off tiptoeing through the tulips, were there some activities, projects (work-related or personal) or some tasks you told yourself you would complete before summer? Well, now is the time to look over that list and get a status of those. Get out your calendar/ planner, walk out into the fresh air and take time for creative thought and planning.

When the month of June ends, half of the year will be behind us. The second quarter of the year will be over and it's important to do a bit of reflection to see if we are where we wanted to be at the halfway mark. If you've been reading this book for a while, having written goals with specific dates of accomplishment is something I've written about before, so see if you are on track with those S.M.A.R.T. goals. If you've recently joined the conversation of wanting to be more energized and efficient, it's never too late to write down specific goals for the rest of the year. But we shouldn't stop there. We have to take those goals, break them down into "next step" activities and schedule them on our calendars, just like our dentist appointments!

Don't despair if you haven't started on specific plans for the year. Whatever you decide, just don't wait until next new year's to begin what you envisioned accomplishing this year!

It's only too late if you never get started!

I always say, "Keep IT moving, whatever the IT is for you."

Continuing our momentum theme for June, it's not only important to keep our dreams, goals and projects moving forward, it's essential for us as humans to keep moving. The research continues to be so strong about what happens with a sedentary lifestyle. Even if we are getting regular moderate exercise or even vigorous exercise, it is not enough, if the rest of our time is spent sitting at a desk, in a chair, or on the couch.

The Centers for Disease Control and Prevention, along with other researchers, suggest that switching even a half-hour of sitting for activity will help.

If we continue to sit and sit, some of the poor health outcomes include increased incidence for diabetes, cardiovascular disease and mortality.

Health experts are suggesting exercising while watching TV, walking during work meetings and even using a stand-up desk or higher counter.

The 150 minutes a week of moderate activity the government suggests will make little to no impact, if the rest of the time we are sitting in our cars, on our couches, or in our chairs.

Let's make a pact to get out there and get moving.

Just start wherever you are, putting one foot in front of the other.

"I am a slow walker, but I never walk back."

– ABRAHAM LINCOLN

"A dream is just a dream. A goal is a dream with a plan and a deadline."

– HARVEY MACKAY

"Some succeed because they are destined to, but others succeed because they are determined to."

– UNKNOWN

"The difference between a successful person and others is not a lack of strength, not a lack of knowledge, but rather a lack in will."

– VINCE LOMBARDI

25. The Power of SELF-DISCIPLINE

I've been enjoying one of Brian Tracy's books, "No Excuses." Brian is a prolific writer, speaker and consultant extraordinaire who has shared his business expertise all over the world. I believe at last count he has spoken in over 75 countries!

Brian lives in the San Diego area and I had the pleasure of meeting him some time back and he graciously wrote a testimonial for me. Perhaps you are familiar with some of his works. One of his most quoted books is called *Eat That Frog!* In it he describes how to attack the biggest project first and just take a bite. If you must eat a big, ugly frog, he posits, do it first and fast!

His book, "No Excuses," is chock-full of wonderful words of wisdom. There are just so many juicy pearls in there. I highly recommend it if you are struggling with self-discipline and you know, deep down, you could be so much more and share more of your gifts with the world.

Below are the Seven Principles of Leadership that Brian identifies in this book. Even if you are not in a leadership position, keep in mind you are leading your life! If you've found yourself getting way off track of the life you want to lead and have, take note of his seven principles:

Clarity - be clear about your goals and objectives - about who you are and what you stand for.

Competence - continually look for ways to improve.

Commitment - are you committed to success and achievement?

Constraints - look at what constraints or limiting factors are holding you back. What resources could you allocate to remove those obstacles?

Creativity - be open to new ideas from a variety of sources. Look for faster, better, and easier ways.

Continuous Learning - Brian is all about lifelong learning. He believes in upgrading one's skills and abilities.

Consistency - can we strive to be reliable, dependable, and predictable? Can we remain positive, calm and confident?

Does one of these seven principles speak to you?

"We all have dreams. But in order to make dreams come into reality, it takes an awful lot of determination, dedication and self-discipline and effort."

- JESSIE OWENS

"I think self-discipline is something; it's like a muscle. The more you exercise it, the stronger it gets."

– DANIEL GOLDSTEIN

"Pursue your dreams with great might."

– LAILAH GIFTY AKITA

"It is often the simple daily practices that influence our lives in dramatic ways."

– ALARIC HUTCHINSON

26. The Power of IN AND OUT DAYS

For some of you in the western United States, your mouth may have started to water after reading the title. I'm not talking about food here, but I sure do love those burgers!

Some of us live in a part of the country where there is a drive-thru/dine-in establishment of tempting delights, and a name like the title above.

I'm not talking about calories, carbohydrates, and clearly delightful eats. No, I'm talking about our schedules—our calendars.

Many of us have responsibilities that take us out of our homes every day, all day—five, six, or seven times a week. Others of us are making several trips in and out of our homes maybe three to five times each day.

If you own your calendar a little bit more than that or would like to, listen up.

Just for a moment, picture you in charge of determining your destinations and when to go here, there, and everywhere.

Visualize a clean slate of a calendar ahead of you. Maybe it's next week or next month. Maybe it's a clear space for tomorrow.

Put yourself in the driver's seat and decide when you want to leave your nest and where you want to go and what you need to do.

Place those "out" responsibilities on one day or part of a day. In other words, when you're out, you're out, and when you're not, you're not.

Gee, maybe there should be a song with that title!

A young mom hired me to help her get organized. She is the CEO of a very busy household, and has a lot of responsibilities and interests.

We took time to examine and evaluate her calendar and routine.

What we uncovered was she was doing a lot of running around and spending enormous amounts of time in the car. By switching up several activities, we were able to find larger blocks of time for focused, concentrated projects she had not been able to get to that she really wanted to do.

This one adjustment to her life brought much-needed peace and calm, and also gave her the time blocks to get to projects she desired.

Many of us are expending way too much time running here or there, even if it's in a car. Freeway fiascoes and commuting conundrums often leave us in such a frenzied state we are no good to anyone else, especially ourselves.

What I'm suggesting here is a bird's-eye view of your calendar over the past week or month. Were there times when you made a trip out of the house and then got back home with less than a half hour to spare and then another trip out?

Did some days feel totally lost and nothing got done that you had planned?

My guess is you were going "in and out" waaay too much.

If you can take some ownership of your days, can you block out time to do "in" projects at home—focused, concentrated, supercharged levels of efficient and effective transformation—and then other days when you plan "out" activities?

Gas station, car wash, post office, dry cleaners, bank, meds pick-up, donation drop-off, medical appointments, hair, nails, business meetings, friend for coffee—all those pesky errand events

Just picture it: you in charge of what gets on the calendar when. Plan your "in" days and "out" days now for next month. Then before making appointments all over the days available make them on the days you plan to be out.

Your in-home productivity will soar, especially if you are running a home-based business. Your energy will increase, and you will find yourself more at peace and more relaxed because now you own the day!

"He is rich who owns the day."
~ Ralph Waldo Emerson

"Success is actually a short race – a sprint fulfilled by discipline just long enough for habit to kick in and take over."

– Gary Keller

27. The Power of PRODUCTIVITY

We are living in the Age of Distraction.

It seems everyone wants a little piece of us, and by continuing to respond to their needs our needs never seem to get met; they end up at the bottom of the laundry basket, sitting quietly, all wrinkled up.

So how do we get more productivity, and get done the dreams and goals that we have?

There certainly isn't any Productivity Store we can go to or order from to gain this limited resource, now is there?

All of us get the same 168 hours per week to attend to everything in our big, beautiful lives. No more and no less. If you've been struggling with getting on with the life you imagine and deserve, it's time to take the reins, establish new habits and create pockets of productivity in your lives.

How?

First, I'm going to suggest looking at your sleep habits. For some of us we are not getting enough sleep, either tossing and turning worrying about too much to do or staying up so late trying to get it all done that we are exhausted the next day and stumble through in a half-zombie state.

For others of us we might be sleeping the day and night away because we are feeling so low and sad about so much to do we have no idea where to start. Either way we are in a lose-lose.

All the current research suggests our bodies and minds need 7-9 hours of sleep nightly. Look at your caffeine intake and the times of day you are consuming caffeine. Do the same with your alcohol intake.

Also, examine the electronic stimulation you are putting your body and mind through right before bedtime. This is important if you are finding yourself restless and unable to shut down the day.

Secondly, is your To-Do List running around in your head and you keep the tape playing because you don't want to forget anything? Time to get it out of there and free up those great brain cells for something more creative.

Use a pad of paper, smart phone, computer, planner, software, whichever suits you to create a Will Do List.

If possible put items in categories, such as phone calls, follow-up, meetings, health, personal; think of categories that match the life you are in right now.

HERE'S THE KEY: Schedule those items into Blocks of Time on your calendar. We schedule appointments with others, why not ourselves? Set a timer for 50 minutes of uninterrupted time and focus on one of those categories.

The secret here is to not to switch-task. What is wearing us out is asking our brains and bodies to multi-task (switch-tasking, really). Ask yourself, "What is the most important thing that I could be doing right now?" Then, focus on just that one task for 50 minutes. If you can go for 90 minutes, do that. Take a 5-10 minute break at the end of a focused 50 minutes.

If you don't think you can stay on one task for 50 minutes, begin with 30-40 minutes and increase from there. The important thing is to just do that one thing, nothing else.

Finally, it's important to stay hydrated and have good healthy snacks at the ready so your brain and body can be alert and focused.

Watch out for "busyness" vs. "productivity."

If you want great results for your efforts, be sure what you are focused on is a high- value activity.

If not, at the end of the day all we have accomplished is rearranging chairs on the Titanic! And we all know how that story ended!

"Each indecision brings its own delays and days are lost lamenting over lost days…What you can do or think you can do, begin it. For boldness has magic, power and genius in it."

– JOHANN WOLFGANG VON GOETHE

"When you start to make things happen, you really begin to believe that you can make things happen. And that makes things happen."

– DAVID ALLEN

Section Three:
July, August, September

28. The Power of EDITING

I'm not an editor - never have been.

And yet, I find myself wearing an editor's hat quite frequently.

Recently, I started writing another book and as much as I am working to not edit my writing as I do my first draft, I catch myself ignoring my advice, and editing a word or a sentence along the way.

That got me thinking about editing on a wider scale.

When working with clients, virtually, I'm really getting them to focus on developing their editing (weeding) skills.

Gardeners are so very good at that - weeding out what's not working, what's crowding out the crown jewels of the gardens so they can see the spectacular. Our lives, offices and homes should be treated like gardens.

Summer lies right before us, like a newly mowed grand lawn of possibilities. In the past, many of us have made mental lists (or written ones) of all sorts of summer projects for the 90 plus days ahead. Some of us have gotten into boasting contests with friends and family as to who has the longest To Do List.

But...the longer list thing rarely works.

May I suggest let's make THIS summer different?

Go ahead - make your **Summer Projects List or Places to Visit List or Parties to Have or People to Meet**. But then, step back, pause, and get out the big pen, the delete button, or the white-out.

And evaluate and

Edit.

What's <u>reasonable</u> to actually accomplish this summer?

With calendar at the ready, with stillness and time to think through all your priorities and possibilities, what would be **BIG WINS** for you this summer?

Think 2-3 items, not 20-30. We need to stop setting ourselves up for failure with the longest TO DO Lists. It's not "He or she with the longest list wins."

It's really quite the opposite.

"My life needs editing."

\- MORT SAHL

"If you have more than three priorities, you have none."

\- JIM COLLINS

"Editing is the essence of writing."

\- TARANG SINHA

29. The Power of CONTROL

Stuff happens.

Things change.

People leave or come into our lives.

As the expression goes, "The only thing we can count on is change."

So how can we feel more in charge of our lives - **more independent** from all the outside clatter chatter - and take back control?

First, we need to analyze if there are areas of our life where we feel out of control. This could be our finances, our health, our environments, the people we associate with, the dreams we have, and so on.

As Jack Canfield, co-creator of Chicken Soup for the Soul Series™, says, "E + R = O." What that means is an Event happens; then comes our Response to that event and that equals the Outcome that occurs. Our response to the stuff that happens becomes the **key** to us leading more successful, productive and happy lives.

So we do need a sense of some control - but not be so controlling that we are rigid and inflexible. It really has to become a bit of a balancing act; we need control but not so much that our creativity and fun get stifled.

Can you control your day?

How about part of your day?

Are there dreams and projects you've been meaning to do but somehow one day turns into another and then another, and those dreams and projects lie dormant in the corners of your mind?

What if you decided to take back control of this one life and put into action some behaviors to move those dreams and projects into fruition?

How would that feel for you?

What would that look like?

Where could you begin?

Start with your calendars/planners to see where has your 168 hours in previous weeks gone. Time is the one equalizer. We all get the same amount. It's what we do with it that separates high performers in the world from people who are just living each day like the previous one, sort of their own version of the movie "Groundhog Day."

In this 21st century many of us seem to be living in the Age of Distraction. We let others' agendas dictate our days (and thus our lives) and rarely move into who we want to become.

Isn't it time to take back control and be an independent thinker and doer of your own life?

What ways could you take back control, starting today?

"Don't seek to control others. Seek to gain greater self-control. Master yourself."

\- UNKNOWN

When you can't control what's happening, challenge yourself to control the way you respond to what's happening. That's where your power is."

\- UNKNOWN

30. The Power of COMPETENCE

Do you want to feel more alive? More accomplished?

If you answered yes, then it's time to challenge yourself with some mini-wins.

Sometimes we can get ourselves into ruts. Our routines and daily habits are so ingrained we just feel like we're going through the motions of each day and not stretching out to learn new skills.

If that sounds like you, think about something you've been putting off doing or even trying for fear of failure, and then one month turns into the next and then the next, and there it is - another year and you never ventured forward to learn that new skill, try that new organization, step into that new adventure.

When that happens, we lose our sense of self-confidence and we tend to hold back. So how can we change that? What can we do?

Let's think in terms of brief wins. In other words if you want to gain more self-confidence and competence in something, set up a 30 Day or 60 Day specific goal of what it could be.

What would you like to be proud of accomplishing? achieving?

Write that down.

Now ask yourself what are the things you need to do between now and then to achieve that? Make it a stretch goal so you are learning something new and strengthening your neural pathways in the brain.

First, ask yourself the important Why question. Why is this goal important to me? What is preventing me from not doing this? What resources or help do I need to make this goal completed in 30-60 days?

Those who are high achievers in the world gain self-confidence and stretch even more by feeling competent and consistently learning new things, thus gaining even more competence and confidence.

Look how far you've come in life so far. That didn't just happen. You made that happen. Be proud and pleased at your achievements and accomplishments. But don't decide you are all done for life, like some baked pie coming out of the oven.

What else do you imagine and dream of?

It's only too late if you never get started!

For inspiration on gaining competence, read Shonda Rimes' book, "Year of Yes" this month.

Ms. Rimes is the prolific writer whose career on ABC brought "Grey's Anatomy", "Private Practice", "Scandal" and "How to Get Away with Murder" and others to TV screens everywhere. Shonda also graduated from the same high school as I, Marian High School, Chicago Heights, IL! I think she really paid attention in English!

> *"The in-box is nothing but a convenient organizing system for other people's agendas."*
> -BRENDON BURCHARD

> *"Sometimes the smallest step in the right direction ends up being the biggest step of your life. Tip toe if you must, but take the step."*
> -UNKNOWN

31. The Power of the MORNING RITUAL

Believe it or not, I love my Morning Ritual!

I can't wait to jump out of bed in the morning and start the new day! To me each day is like a box of new crayons or a big, blank white board of possibility. Over the years I have revised and improved my Morning Ritual and now it's just plain fun!

Is it perfect every morning? No.

Are there some mornings where I miss one of these? Yes.

Does it center me for the start of a fabulous day? Absolutely!

Here are My TOP FIVE ROUTINES:

#1 Roll over off the bed and onto my knees (2-3 minutes)

And thank God for another day to get it "right." I didn't always have this in a morning routine but since putting it there, first thing, I have the opportunity to focus on gratitude and appreciation for my many blessings.

#2 Make the bed (3-4 minutes)

Even if the day falls apart later, I feel a great sense of accomplishment with this simple act. I've been sharing this step with many coaching clients over the years. From a de-cluttering/organizing perspective, the bed takes up 80% of the bedroom, so this one act can bring calm, peace and tranquility to your bedroom sanctuary.

In May 2014 retired Adm. William H. McRaven gave a commencement address at his alma mater, University of Texas. That speech can be viewed online (search William McRaven University of Texas Commencement Speech). The graduating seniors so loved his talk that it has now been viewed more than 10 million times. In essence he told them "If you want to change the world, start off by making your bed." Adm. McRaven has expanded that talk into a little book, "Make Your Bed - Little Things That Can Change Your Life...And Maybe the World."

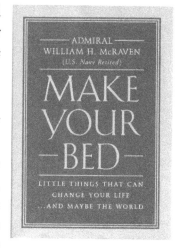

#3 Hydrate (1-2 minutes)

I drink 10 ounces of water right away after waking.

"Think of water as a nutrient your body needs that is present in liquids, plain water, and foods. All of these are essential daily to replace the large amounts of water lost each day," says Joan Koelemay,

#4 Slap on My Fitbit as I read an inspirational quote for the day. (<1 minute)

This year I've been reading the Louise Hay quote on her daily tear-off lifestyles calendar. Louise passed away at the age of 90 in 2017 after a life that started with much hardships but moved into high achievement. She is the founder of Hay House, a publishing company with many inspirational books.

#5 Stretching, arm circles, and wall push-ups (10 minutes)

I love this step! This wakes me up for the day. I bend and stretch and reach and stretch; I spin my arms every direction with arms extended. Then I lean against a wall and do several push-ups.

I encourage each of you to revisit your morning routine and evaluate how it's working (or not) for you. No one needs to follow my Morning Ritual. I just wanted to share how it frames the first part of my day for better productivity, calm and focus!

And isn't that what most of us are craving?

Here's to Magical Mornings for you!

Don't have a Morning Ritual that's working for you?

What can you **COMMIT** to putting in place starting tomorrow morning?

"Up until now."

– LILA LARSON

"Take your life in your own hands and what happens?
A terrible thing: no one is to blame. "

– ERICA JONG

"Think more of yourself, and demand that your actions be
congruent with the best of who you are and who you can be."

BRENDON BURCHARD

32 The Power of the FINISH LINE

The seasons pass by so quickly it seems. Then we are left with memories and moments to remember.

If you've ever watched the Olympics, Winter or Summer, you've witnessed these moments. The Olympics occur every four years, and with it we have the opportunity to see people who have had big dreams, goals and aspirations - many of them since they were young children.

If you had a chance to follow the stories of some of the athletes you might have marveled at how they overcame tremendous odds to reach the pinnacle in their particular sport. Not a single one of them was "an overnight sensation." Each of them set a destination - a goal - and then "backward mapped" it to reach the Olympic level.

We can all learn from the behaviors of the athletes: the good, the bad, and the ugly. Let's focus on the good ones here.

Below are TEN TAKE-AWAYS:

1. Be prepared.
2. Stay focused.
3. When you stumble, get right back up.
4. When things don't go as planned, let go of what you dreamed and adjust to what is.
5. Visualize your success.
6. Create a positive mindset.
7. Persevere.
8. Help others when you can.
9. Relish in your victories, no matter how big or how small.
10. Thank those who helped you along the way.

"Have enough courage to start and enough heart to finish."

– JESSICA YOURKO

"Life is like riding a bicycle. In order to keep your balance, you need to keep moving."

– ALBERT EINSTEIN

"You must take personal responsibility. You cannot change the circumstances, the seasons of the wind, but you can change yourself."

– JIM ROHN

33. The Power of INDEPENDENCE

As we celebrate the birthday of our country, let's take a moment to think back to our history books about Independence Day. The people who were fighting for freedom and independence from England's rule endured a lot of hardships and harrowing experiences, but they never gave up; they persevered.

Today we enjoy living in a country that has so many freedoms, because of the efforts of these courageous folks. However you celebrate the 4th of July, whether it's at a picnic in the park, a parade in town, or watching fireworks in person or on television, I hope you expand your Independence Day to Independence Month.

Being independent means being free from outside control, so this makes July the perfect month to look at our stuff and the control it may have over us. Take a look around you. Are you in control of your stuff or is it controlling you?

If your life, home or business world has become so cluttered that you cannot enjoy your space and are unable to find the things you need when you need them, then you are not living a life of independence!

July is the perfect time to decide no more. It's time we stop complaining about our spaces and/or lack thereof and start taking action and clearing up the places we do have. I just finished working on Jack Canfield's Assisting Team all last week as he presented the mid-year week of his Train the Trainer Program. I know most of you know who he is, but just in case someone out there can't recall, he is the co-creator of the Chicken Soup for the Soul® Series, and author of "The Success Principles," and a star in the hit movie, "The Secret."

Being around Jack Canfield for an entire week, as one of his assistants, is always inspirational for me, and last week was no different.

While each training day was packed with assignments to support Jack and his work, I returned home more motivated than ever to continue incorporating his success principles into my work and daily living experiences.

Jack's first principle in "The Success Principles" is Take 100% Responsibility for Your Life. It is the foundation of all of the other principles in his book and teachings. He reiterated this cornerstone principle so well this past week in Scottsdale, Arizona.

We have to stop complaining and stop blaming and take a good, hard look at the decisions we are making. If our world has become not a happy one, it's up to us to make changes in it, and create a different outcome.

Our founding fathers wanted to create an environment so that people in their generation and all future generations could have life, liberty and the pursuit of happiness. Now it's up to us!

"You are not your stuff."
– PETER WALSH

"Treasure your relationships, not your possessions."
– ANTHONY J. D'ANGELO

"Of all possessions a friend is the most precious."
– HERODOTUS

34. The Power of a S.Y.S.T.E.M.

Even though we are still in the throes of summer (Yippee!), it's always smart to look ahead and think how one can be more efficient and energized once fall rolls around. To me the new year has always started in the fall; this is from a lifetime of going to school and working in schools for many years. I know for many of you the new year doesn't start until the ball drops on New Year's Eve but that hasn't been the case for me.

Summer has a different rhythm to it than the rest of the year, a somewhat slower pace with longer days and what seems like more minutes to each day. It's also the ideal time to do some strategic planning for September. If your household is full of youngsters of various ages and sizes, now is the time to go through those closets and cupboards and find out what still fits, what still works and what needs to be released to the universe (or at least to smaller relatives).

Parents, take a look at your children's bedrooms and see if they are set up for great nights of sleep once the school year begins. Inventory the supplies you have on hand to make that first week and first month back to school a most successful start.

For those of you without children in the home, think what systems you can put in place so easing out of summer will not be too painful. You do know what S.Y.S.T.E.M. stands for, yes?

Save Yourself Some Time Energy & Money

Take a few minutes and think about what in your life could you systematize for greater efficiency and more energy. If you're not sure where to start, here are some examples: your morning routine, your evening ritual before turning out the lights, your clothes closet and drawers for faster dressing in the morning, your schedule/calendar/

planner, your errands routine, your world of work, your route to work, your grocery shopping, your home office routines, your fitness schedule, your meal prep, your kitchen clean-up, etc.

Evaluate the above areas in your life and see if they could use some tweaking before summer stops and autumn appears.

"Everything must be made as simple as possible. But not simpler."

— ALBERT EINSTEIN

"Organization isn't about perfection; it's about efficiency, reducing stress and clutter, saving time and money and improving your overall quality of life."

— CHRISTINA SCALISE

"The point of simple living for me has got to be: a soft place to land, a wide margin of error, room to breathe, lots of places to find baseline happiness in each and every day."

— LEO BABAUTA

"He who does not get fun and enjoyment out of every day…needs to reorganize his life."

— GEORGE M. ADAMS

35. The Power of WEEDING

It all started when I thought I needed to get more hangers for my closet.

For some reason, all of a sudden there seemed to be a major shortage of hangers to be found. As I was starting to create a list of what else was needed before I went out into the world, I stopped myself...

And remembered what I had said to one of my wonderful clients earlier in the year. Let's call her Julie. On that particular day she and I had been attacking paper piles, and whittling them away. As I was leaving I said to Julie if you can schedule some time this coming week, it would be great to set up a "weeding time" on your calendar and attack one or two of the file drawers in your home office.

I went on to explain that just like great gardeners need to weed their gardens from time to time so that the flowers and plants have breathing room, all of us need to give our files some room to breathe and de- clutter what no longer serves us.

I stood at my closet entrance and thought: I bet all the hangers I need are in here being used for items I no longer wear. Without a major closet overhaul I hired myself for the morning, worked quickly and pulled out tops and bottoms I had not worn in a very long time. The better garments got set aside to drop off at a consignment store later in the week when I was with an "Out" block of time. Other items went into a large bag for donation to an agency I support in town.

What I had been avoiding since the last time I organized my closet I faced head-on: I tried on every pair of slacks and crop pants in there. Before I started this part I took a deep breath, put on some dancing music, gave myself a limited amount of time and got working.

Like a good gardener I kept weeding and weeding. My collection of 12 pairs of black pants got reduced to four, four that I will actually wear, rather than just taking up valuable real estate in my closet.

With bags removed from the bedroom and brought downstairs I took a look at my leftover hangers: TWELVE, plus additional ones that I used for pants.

Perfect.

No need to go out and buy more hangers.

"Everyone has enough weeding to do in their own garden."

– FLEMISH PROVERB

"Be careful what you water your dreams with. Water them with worry and fear and you will produce weeds that choke the life from your dream. Water them with optimism and solutions, and you will cultivate success. Always be on the lookout for ways to turn a problem into an opportunity for success. Always be on the lookout for ways to nurture your dream."

– LAO TZU

36. The Power of VOLUNTEERING

In 2005 during the Labor Day weekend, I watched the devastating news on television about Hurricane Katrina. It's hard to believe how many years ago that happened because the memory of that weekend and the weeks following are etched so clearly in my mind.

With winds of 127 mph many of us could not believe the horror and fear in the eyes of the people of New Orleans as the hurricane broke through a defective levee system flooding 4/5 of the city.

Watching people on rooftops, hoping to escape from their flooded homes and crying out for help consumed me that weekend. For those who could reach the Louisiana Superdome the conditions were deplorable and the place was not fit for human beings. That this was all happening in our country, not some far off land, was mind-blowing to me and many others.

\While financial donations were pouring in throughout that weekend and beyond, I realized writing a check to a first-responder agency was not enough for me. I immediately contacted the American Red Cross and took part in enough specific training that I was able to deploy to Louisiana for two weeks of volunteer service. Once there I interviewed and assisted families to get them immediate resources so that they could begin to rebuild their lives.

Years later there is still much work to be done there, though there has been a great deal of rebuilding. There were 1,400 people who lost their lives and thousands more who lost their livelihoods and their homes. The experience of helping others in need was a very powerful one for me; it got me out of "me" and quickly over to "them" - what did they need, how could I be of service to them, and how could I help reduce their pain and discomfort.

I write this today not to take any accolades as there were thousands of volunteers working throughout this disaster and who continue to do great work for first-responder agencies all the time. Rather, I want all of us to take a pause from our busy, hectic lives for a moment and think about others. To give to those in need it isn't necessary to leave the area or your state.

Think about what places are there in your community that could use some help: your local school, a nearby library, a senior center or a hospital, to name just a few. Often, we think we need to wait until our calendars are completely blank or everything in our lives is all tidied up, but the truth is, that rarely happens.

Just for a few minutes sit still and think about some who are less fortunate than you. Do you have a few hours each month to share your talents and skills?

Do you love to read? Share your love of reading with a child by becoming a tutor. Ask at your local library or school how you can help.

"Just Do It."

– NIKE

"I am only one, but I am one. I cannot do everything, but I can do something. And I will not let what I cannot do interfere with what I can do."

– EDWARD EVERETT HALE

"Help one another; there's no time like the present and no present like the time."

– JAMES DURST

37. The Power of SIMPLICITY

As our days get shorter and our nights start earlier, it's time to shift our attention from the outdoors back inside to our environments: our homes and our work spaces. We continue to live in an Age of Distraction with too many decisions to make because of information overload. This month let's take a look at what we could simplify in our lives and in our environment to create more calm and less chaos.

In a previous chapter I talked about the power of creating a S.Y.S.T.E.M. in some of your daily activities (saving yourself some time, energy and money). If you haven't had a chance to put some new systems in place, now is a good time to revisit that.

We often feel on overwhelm because we are overloaded with too many choices, too many distractions, too many shiny objects that say "buy me," "try me," or "get this today and your life will be great."

Instead of those things bringing us pleasure we often become burdened by them, leading to overwhelm, as we find these new items cluttering up our lives, our homes and our minds.

This month what could you simplify that could lead to more calm and happiness for you? What could you eliminate from your world that really isn't all that essential? What is clogging up your life and environments? What have you made so complicated that it is no longer bringing you joy and happiness?

By September 23 there will be only 100 days left in the year. What goals did you set last January and are you on track to finish the year with those complete? If not, in what ways could you simplify some routines so you could get those projects, goals and aspirations kicked into high gear so the year finishes strong for you?

Even small steps are a great beginning.

"The greatest step toward a life of simplicity is to learn to let go."
–STEVE MARABOLI

"Our life is frittered away by detail. Simplify, simplify."
– HENRY DAVID THOREAU

"Life is really simple, but we insist on making it complicated."
– CONFUCIUS

"It's not a daily increase, but a daily decrease.
Hack away at the unessentials."
– BRUCE LEE

38. The Power of ROUTINES

It's almost fall and time to look forward to tighter routines and schedules as well as a strong finish for the year. We are moving toward the autumn of the year, and with it it's time for a little reflection on the goals you set back in January. Was this the year you were going to: move, change jobs, retire, start a business or find that significant someone? How did you do? Take a moment to review your S.M.A.R.T. goals for this year, and see if you are on track to make a fabulous finale to the year.

Hopefully, your goals have been written down and are so specific that you are able to measure their progress quite succinctly. Maybe you didn't get them down on paper but know them by heart; perhaps they were simply to clear the garage, or get rid of a relationship that you know in your heart is not healthy and not working for you. Maybe it was to get a degree or take some classes to learn a new skill.

Whatever you dreamed of having happen in the bright new beginnings of January, I want you to visualize that there still is time to make those dreams a reality.

But... you need a plan of specifics. One cannot sit in a room in the lotus position with eyes closed waiting for miracles. There are over 120 days left in the year. Stop and ask yourself what can you make happen that you have been putting off?

There are over 2,800 hours left this year. Look at your calendar now and schedule in some You Time to get moving on turning those dreams into actionable steps to success. One way to do this is look at the givens and commitments you already have. Can you get those into more of a routine so they become second nature to you by using checklists or streamlining the steps? Maybe you could delegate some of these tasks or decide how important they are to your overall vision of a fabulous year.

Create possibilities in your schedule for what is really important to you. When clients and seminar participants tell me they simply don't have any time to get to what THEY really want to accomplish, I say it's time to make YOUR goals a priority.

Do a time log for a week and see where your time is going. Keep a log at 30-60 minute intervals. Record the task, time and interruptions. See if you are the one causing the lack of focus.

Examine and evaluate what you found out about your habits and routines. Do you get lost in emails? Are you surfing the net, checking up on Facebook friends, or wandering away and avoiding what's right in front of you that needs your complete undivided attention and FOCUS?

By tightening your schedule and creating better habits you'll find you have taken back more of your life than ever before, giving you the gift of a fantastic, focused fall!

"You can either take action or hang back and hope for a miracle. Miracles are great, but they are so unpredictable."
– PETER DRUCKER

"You gotta have a dream. If you don't have a dream, how you gonna have a dream come true?"
–FROM SOUTH PACIFIC, "HAPPY TALK"

39. The Power of HOLIDAY PLANNING AND PREPARATION!

Bet that got your attention, didn't it? Early fall is the absolute best time to think ahead and visualize the last two months of the year. Get out your calendar now and let's do a little backward mapping. As the late, great Stephen Covey used to say, "Begin with the End in Mind." This is one of his seven habits of highly effective people. I want you to have a fantastic finish to the year so let's focus together on making that happen.

I LOVE mindmaps. I hope you do, too. They are way more fun than any kind of outline you may have done in school, either for an assignment or a test. There are some great, free mindmap software programs on the internet. You can also buy upgrades if you want something more elaborate. If neither of these ideas are an option you want, simply grab a piece of paper and a pen or pencil, and let's get going.

Make a sketch similar to the picture below. I like paper that is at least 8.5 x 11, if not larger, but I have also made very effective and useful mindmaps in small notepads.

In the center of yours put the word "Holidays." Now, pause and think about what you really want to have happen this holiday season, letting go of perfect and focusing on possible.

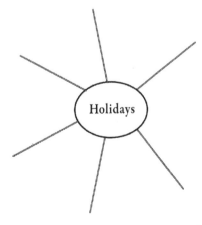

Use the mindmap to discern the main areas for you this coming holiday season. Each person's mindmap will be a bit different, reflective of their beliefs, traditions and family customs.

On the spokes of the wheel put the big categories for you. Perhaps you are the one who does a big gathering during the holidays. If so, put the date of that in the center and think of all the categories, such as menu, guest list, house prep, invitations. You want to get out of your head as soon as possible the main pieces of this project, so you are not worrying and stewing and trying to keep it all upstairs. Give your brain a break!

Maybe you are not the Perle Mesta for family or friends, but there are many different activities and events that occur in your life from November 1- December 31st. Put one event at the end of each spoke and feel free to add more spokes if necessary. Here are some ideas: gift ideas, religious traditions, home decor, holiday cards, any get-togethers. Add ones that fit your world.

As your brain starts to release the subsets of the above areas, simply add lines coming out from the spokes. For example, a spoke of gift ideas would have lines underneath for those I normally get gifts and included would be some ideas or sizes or price points. Getting this info out of my head and onto something tangible opens up more space in my brain for other higher level thinking skills, unrelated to this project.

While you're thinking of holidays, fall is the perfect time to update your database. Whether or not you send out traditional holiday cards makes no difference. This is what I call the once a year "jiffy tune-up list" of friends, family and folks you want to continue connections.

*"Let your heart be your compass, your mind your map,
your soul your guide ... and you will never get lost."*

– Rita Ghatourey

"A goal without a plan is just a wish."

– Antoine de Saint-Exupery

40. The Power of the START

Often my clients are stuck on where to **start** to de-clutter their life and get on with the life they imagine and deserve. Recently, one of my clients was feeling absolutely overwhelmed with so much getting in the way and blocking her success and dreams.

Whether it's virtually or in person, once I see the environment that has put my coaching client into so much stress, I can easily pick a starting place. However, I have to say when I viewed this particular client's environment and saw what the problems were, even I was perplexed for a few minutes about a starting point.

There were **so many places we could choose!**

We both took a few deep breaths and I made a decision -

A decision to start with the refrigerator! I know it may sound counterintuitive to you that with so much "visual noise" surrounding her environment that I would pick something hidden and "behind the scenes."

But it worked!

By starting small in this one contained area this mini-project had boundaries (the refrigerated items were all together and not all over the house); the decisions came quickly and efficiently (expired, moldy food had to go), and categories were so simple to discern (fruits from dairy, from vegetables, etc).

Done in less than 30 minutes this client was beaming and feeling like she was starting to take back control…and ready to tackle another mini-project!

And that's really key -

taking back control of the one life we have —one step at a time —one day at a time!

Guaranteed!

"Once you replace negative thoughts with positive ones you'll start having positive results."

- WILLIE NELSON

"Start by doing what's necessary, then do what's possible, and suddenly you are doing the impossible."

- ST. FRANCIS OF ASSISI

"Your present circumstances don't determine where you can go; they merely determine where you start."

- NIDO QUBEIN

41. The Power of FALLING BACK HOME

For those of us in Southern California it never seems like fall until November. The months of September and October are spectacularly summery, except that the tourists have left town, leaving us with more elbow room. Often, it's hard to get into the autumn of the year until we turn back our clocks to Standard Time and the nights and early mornings become quite cool. With our sunsets now at 5 p.m. it's wonderful to hurry home from the day and get nested inside and off the freeways.

Dorothy said it best: "There's no place like home." Whether you are having company for Thanksgiving, going to someone else's house, or having a quiet holiday at home, this is the perfect time to take a look at your nest.

Focus on the public places. Pretend you are seeing them for the first time. If you have no idea where to start, begin at the front door.

Can you put up a fall wreath on the door? How about some pumpkins, gourds, welcoming pilgrims or dried floral arrangements? Maybe switching out a summery welcome mat for something with fall leaves, perhaps.

Autumn is the perfect time for scented candles that can bring apple spices, cinnamon, pumpkin and other yummy flavors into your home, but without the added calories.

If your front door already looks fabulous for fall, move on to the foyer of your home. The best way to create a new scheme is to empty the space as best as you can. Sometimes this is impossible if you live alone. If that is the case, clear the counter tops and move the items out of the room, at least temporarily.

Once you've cleared the space, give it a thorough cleaning. This will create new energy for the mouth of your home and get you ready to rebuild the space for the holidays.

Add back the largest items first. Perhaps it's a large vase that you have. What can you put in it to reflect the season? Do you have table runners, accessories or Thanksgiving décor? Take some time and rebuild the space. When you have finished, walk out and come back in, pretending you are viewing it for the very first time. Now is the time to do some editing and tweaking. This is where I often remove an item or two or move something to a different location.

Do these above steps in your living/family rooms and dining spaces and you will create a nurturing nest for you and yours.

"He is a wise man who does not grieve for the things which
he has not, but rejoices for those which he has."

- Epictetus

"Feeling grateful or appreciative of someone or something in your life actually
attracts more of the things that you appreciate and value into your life."

- Christine Northrup

Section Four:
October, November, December

42. The Power of PERSEVERANCE

Perseverance can be very powerful if we just start with one small change of habit and build from that. Often, however, many of us give up too easily. There are about 90 days of the year left for us to clear up some leftovers, fulfill our goals for the year and get on with creating the life we imagine and deserve. Put on your thinking cap – what could you focus on for the next 90 days to complete the year with a streamlined, productive and happy finish?

It's only too late, if we don't start.

Many of you have probably heard of the story in Napoleon Hill's book, "Think and Grow Rich." In that book he tells the story of R. U. Harby.

Many years ago Harby had an uncle who had gold fever. So what did he do? He staked a claim and he started digging. The uncle worked very hard and finally found a vein of ore. He covered up his find, and then went home to raise the money for the machines needed to bring the ore to the surface.

Once the money was raised, Darby went with his uncle back to his claim to make their fortune. Soon, they had enough to pay off their debts. They were excited because they knew now everything else would be pure profit!

But…bad luck found them. The gold supply stopped. That one vein of ore had disappeared.

They kept on going; kept on digging.

Alas, they found nothing.

After some time they were so frustrated that they quit and sold all their machinery for a few hundred dollars to a junk man.

Darby and his uncle went home, so frustrated and disappointed.

What did the junk man do? He contacted a mining engineer who checked out the mine and determined that there was another vein of gold just THREE FEET from where Darby and his uncle had stopped digging.

That smart junk man?

He went on to make millions from the mine.

What about Darby? He went home, paid off all the folks who had loaned him money and became determined to learn from the mistake of giving up too soon.

Darby became a very successful insurance salesman. He more than recouped what he would have made from the gold mine, learning the lesson of persevering through difficult times and staying focused if you want to become successful.

Don't give up on your dreams.

You may be just three feet from gold!

> *"Many of life's failures are people who did not realize how close they were to success when they gave up...I have not failed. I've just found 10,000 ways that won't work."*
>
> - THOMAS EDISON

> *"There is no elevator to success. You have to take the stairs."*
>
> – AUTHOR UNKNOWN

> *"Decide what you want; decide what you are willing to exchange for it. Establish your priorities and go to work."*
>
> – RANDY PAUSCH

> *"To fight fear, act. To increase fear – wait, put off, postpone."*
>
> – DAVID JOSEPH SCHWARTZ

> *"Perseverance is not a long race; it is many short races one after the other."*
>
> – WALTER ELLIOTT

43. The Power of TRICKING YOURSELF INTO ACTION

With the holidays creeping quickly upon us, sometimes we get so frightened of all that we have to do (or want to do) for the holiday season, we reach a state of paralysis. There's so much to add to an already busy schedule, we think how can we possibly survive (and thrive) during this busy time of year.

Often, we spend more time stirring in our own juices of negative self-talk or "should-ing" on ourselves that we can get worked up into a real hornet's nest. Let's take the mystery out of all our obligations so our thoughts don't haunt us night and day.

How to do this?

1. Get whatever is stirring around in your head out of there. Using whatever means works best for you, write or type what's been chatting at you, gnawing at you, or keeping you bewitched and bewildered-all the obligations, deadlines, extravagant plans and possibilities that you would love to happen between now and New Year's Eve.

2. With calendar in hand backward map each event or project. In other words get those deadlines down where you can see them and then break the large projects into reasonable chunks. Calendar in as many sub-steps as possible, and hold to that time as best you can.

3. Have a giant project that you know you need to start but you keep looking for a big block of blank space in your schedule and it just hasn't appeared? Guess what? It's not going to show up like magic.

4. Instead, take one bite of that project and calendar that activity. The important question to ask ourselves is this: "What one

thing could I do next that would get that project moving?" Maybe it's a phone call. Maybe it's 20 minutes of thinking time. Maybe it's contacting someone by email or it's one-3 hour activity block.

5. What could you do to trick yourself into some action today?
6. Sometimes our imaginations run away with us and make things much more frightening and daunting than they are. By taking just one small step in the direction of our goals, we recognize that the only thing holding us back is our own fears and perceptions.
7. So, get mapping out your Plan of Action for the remainder of the year, and schedule in time to work your plan.
8. Put small treats in along the way to encourage little victories of success. These don't have to be high in calorie at all: 10 minutes with a favorite magazine, 20 minutes with a walk in nature, 60 minutes with a massage, haircut or trip to the nail salon. The important thing is to recall the power of the reward! We all want treats of some kind from time to time-regardless of our age!

"Prior proper planning prevents poor performance."

– BETTY SWEENEY

"Decide what you want, review it constantly, and each day do something that moves you toward those goals."

– JACK CANFIELD

"Be glad of life because it gives you a chance to love and to work and to play and to look up at the stars."

– HENRY VAN DYKE

44. The Power of a ZEN OFFICE SPACE

Many of us work from home these days. Even if you are not running a business from home there is still the business of your world of paperwork, bill paying, files and being the CEO of your life. Today's busy homeowner has a computer, printer, and a variety of paperwork and files at home. Those who are business owners or busy executives have work files and business-related items to manage at home as well.

Ask yourself:

How is your space looking these days?

Do you have a designated home office space or are you having to work from a kitchen or dining room table? Is this area conducive to productivity and focus or are you easily distracted and unable to get much done quickly?

If you are not pleased with the work space at home, schedule time to address those issues so you can move into the twilight of the year with a better sense of calm, purpose and productivity. The holidays can then be a time of focus on family, friends and religious traditions, and you can enjoy them more knowing the business side of your life is in great shape.

Here are some steps to get you focused on a better home office environment:

1. Look around your work space and take it all in, like you've never seen it before. Does it show a clutter-free, organized environment that looks like a great place to get work done?
2. Is everything out because the drawers and cupboards are packed with too many items and things that may have lost

their usefulness?

3. Do all of your office items have a designated home or will any counter top do, which leads you to wasted time because you are looking for things?

4. Grab some bankers boxes and magic markers, and schedule a date with yourself to focus on bringing down the visual noise.

5. Rest up the night before the date. Have water and protein ready. Turn off your cell phone and get started!

6. Label the boxes: Take to another room, Shred, Toss, Donate, Recycle, Trash, File, Action, and Read.

7. Set a timer and work for 50 minutes right in that space. Do NOT go wandering about, like returning things to other rooms. This will get you off task, distracted and worn out! I know this for a fact because that's the way I used to try and get organized.

8. At the end of the 50 minutes, do a happy dance, take a 10 minute restroom/refreshment/break and decide if you can stay focused for another block of time.

9. Repeat above steps, scheduling on your calendar when you can return. Reward yourself at the end of the great day of de-cluttering and focus.

The holidays are just around the corner - here they come! I want you to be ready to enjoy them!

"Happiness is a very small desk and a very big wastebasket."
–ROBERT ORBEN

"Even though you're growing up, you should never stop having fun."
– NINA DOBREV

"Stuff that's hidden and murky and ambiguous is scary because you don't know what it does."
– JERRY GARCIA

45. The Power of MAKING ROOM

Make ROOM for the HOLIDAYS! Ready or not, here they come. Some folks love the holidays while others face them with dread and desperation. Start now to plan the perfect November-December ever!

Make ROOM in your refrigerator for upcoming company get-togethers. Be ruthless and rugged with determination to clean out the refrigerator and freezer of items that may have been sitting in there way too long.

Make ROOM in your closet for the cooler weather and possible clothing purchases or gifts. Now is the time to clear out items in your closet that you are no longer wearing, that no longer fit, that you no longer enjoy.

Donate them to a worthwhile cause and let the clothes and shoes that you really love have room to breathe. Any clothing and shoes that you are no longer wearing can be donated. Think of an agency you support and either drop off the items or arrange for a pick up.

Make ROOM in your calendar now and schedule your must-do holiday events. Delete activities that you no longer enjoy and plan special evenings at home with loved ones or just yourself. Sometimes it's creating the "Not to Do" list for the holiday season that can keep us sane during this busy time of year.

Make ROOM in your heart for gratitude. Do you know a veteran you can thank for their service today? We have so much to be thankful for this Thanksgiving. Start a Gratitude List and see how many people and things you are grateful to have in your life. I started my list and so far I've got: a small, but mighty family, a strange dog who needed a home, the perfect house, rain on the best days, a car I love, a weight I can live with, plenty of clothes and shoes, veterans past and present who keep us safe, a growing business, and opportunities to do what I love.

What's on your Gratitude List?

*"You must clear out what you don't want to make
room for what you do want to arrive."*

- BRYANT MACGILL

"The biggest room in the world is the room for improvement."

- HELMUT SCHMIDT

*"Resolve to let go of everything that isn't making your life better,
sweeter, and richer, so you can make room for everything that does."*

- UNKNOWN

46. The Power of SCHEDULES

As our days get shorter and our nights seem longer, it's time to turn ourselves inward a bit and look at where our time goes. Whether we are a believer of the "tight schedule" or the "loose - I'll think about doing that tomorrow," either way, our days become weeks and our weeks become months and then years.

Sometimes when we begin new years we have all sorts of visions of what we plan to accomplish for the year. Many of us get on and do exactly what we set out to do, while others of us just have those ideas as dreams and fleeting thoughts. Some of us even have the very best intentions and put our goals into actionable steps to success, but are met with roadblocks along the way that we had no control over.

My mentor and friend, Jack Canfield, co-creator of the #1 New York Times best-selling Chicken Soup for the Soul® series and author of "The Success Principles," refers to those challenging times as getting off course. It doesn't mean we need to abandon our goals; it just means we have to get them back "on course."

Now is the perfect time of the year to look at **schedules**. For those of you with children at home, you have already had to put schedules back on to the front burner. School and sports activities along with music lessons and clubs dictate the fall schedules in many households. The rest of us need to take note and be just as aware and clear as to where our time goes.

Scheduling time to actually do what's important in your life FIRST can be very freeing. Taking time to study our calendars and commitments can help all of us recognize that time is really a limited resource - we all get the same amount.

I recommend "batch to the max" - putting like tasks together and knocking them out in a time block. That might be a group of phone calls or bills to pay or emails to answer. It's single-tasking, but all the tasks are of the same kind.

Getting routines established and reinforced can create more breathing space in one's calendar and life as well. The more automatic and routine we can make certain tasks the faster and easier they will be to complete.

What items on your "will do" list have you been able to get automated by putting into a routine?

"The key is not to prioritize what's on your schedule, but to schedule your priorities."

-STEPHEN COVEY

"One look at an email can rob you of 15 minutes of focus. One call on your cell phone, one tweet, one instant message can destroy your schedule, forcing you to move meetings or blow off really important things like love and friendship."

-JACQUELINE LEO

"You don't have to work for Google or any of the other firms encouraging staff to pursue personal projects on company time, to use slowness to unlock your creativity. Anyone can do it. Start by clearing space in your schedule for rest, daydreaming and serendipity. Take breaks away from your desk, especially when you get stuck on a problem."

-CARL HONORE

"Don't fit the tasks into your schedule; rather schedule tasks into designated blocks of time."

-SUE CRUM

47. The Power of DECIDING

I think one of the best skills we can develop as people who want to be high performers and people who achieve their dreams and goals is the ability to make decisions...

and then move on.

Throughout the course of a day all of us are making decisions from the moment we wake up, before even getting out of bed until the very end when the lights go out.

As adults we make about 35,000 remotely conscious decisions each day, depending on our responsibilities. Children make about 3,000 daily decisions. According to researchers at Cornell University (Wansink and Sobal, 2007), we are making 226.7 decisions each day on just food!

You might be asking why making decisions is such a focus, and why I'm even mentioning it today.

Good question.

It's really the decisions we make on a daily basis that form our lifetime habits.

Decisions can be big or small. Where to live or what to eat for breakfast. Who to marry or not. What clothes to put on for the day. What career to pursue or whether to check Facebook before getting out of bed.

See - there are all kinds of decisions.

When we arrive at the end of our life and if we're lucky enough to have time to reflect back, it will be our decisions that made the difference for us. Those forks in the road, when we could go here or there, or become this or that, or live near or far, or travel or not—will

be viewed as the turning points in our lives.

Decision-making can be easy, like, what's for dinner tonight.

And the next one right behind it can be hard - to stay or go, to play small or big, to step outside our comfort zone or remain inside what we know so well.

As far as I know, we only get this ONE BIG LIFE. If that's the case then we really have only one decision to make —to play small or to play big. Once we decide on that everything else starts to fall into place.

John Assaraf, author, star in "The Secret," has said it so well when he says, "Are you interested or are you committed? If you're interested, you'll do what's convenient. If you're committed, you'll do what it takes."

When we make those big decisions in life, we have to check in with our heart vs. our head. How does it **feel**? Will this big decision **expand my life** or **will it contract it**?

Often, coaching clients ask me how to decide to get rid of certain things. They want me to decide for them. They say it's just too difficult to make the decision. My response is always the same. One has to start with the easier decisions: the old catalogs and magazines, the clothes that don't fit, the people that drain you of all positive energy, and the over-scheduled calendar.

Make decisions there first.

Get in the habit of deciding and see that you are still breathing and alive on the other side of the decision. Never start with the emotional, memory clutter. Start far away from that in the beginning. When you are ready for that, you will have already practiced on the non-essential, the non-important and non-emotional stuff that's been clogging you.

As many of you know I love and live to snow ski. As our weather here this week has gone from 104 degrees at the beach (unheard of before) to a rainy, cool Halloween, there's snow in the mountains with our ski mountain opening in just NINE days for the new season. When we skiers and snowboarders are standing at the top of a run, we have to make the decision as to when to "**drop in**." The pitch of the run, the weather and the number of people on the run are all factors that run through one's mind before deciding when to drop in.

I have watched many people really struggle with dropping in, and I, too, have stood at the top of some ski runs with great reserve about dropping in at just the right moment.

Here's the thing: once you let go and "lean in" to it, the decision is made and the next action steps appear. As my dear friend and mentor Jack Canfield always says, "You don't need to see every turn of the highway when you start on a long journey. You just need to know the next part of the road."

Wishing you a great road ahead!

"Most of my failures can be ascribed to the fact that I chose that which was 'easy' over that which was 'right.' And while it's right to admit this to myself, it isn't easy. So which choice am I going to make this time?"

-CRAIG D. LOUNSBROUGH

"Focus is a matter of deciding what things you're not going to do."

-JOHN CARMACK

"The key is taking responsibility and initiative, deciding what your life is about and prioritizing your life around the most important things."

-STEPHEN COVEY

48. The Power of MORE GRATITUDE

*"This nation will remain the land of the free only
so long as it is the home of the brave."*

- ELMER DAVIS

As I write this it is Veterans Day. It is time to pause and be grateful for the freedoms we have, and thank the people who have made sacrifices to keep us free. There is so much we have to be grateful for: a roof over our heads, some food for our bellies, a few friends we can count on, and maybe some family members we cherish deeply.

You might be thinking that I wrote about gratitude at the beginning of this book, and you would be correct. However, if we can bookend each year with gratitude or better yet, bookend our days with it, we can live at a higher frequency.

November is the perfect time to look around our home and see its abundance. If we've been complaining about our "stuff," such as closets bursting with too many clothes, perhaps we can schedule some short bursts of de-cluttering and get some items ready for donation to our favorite charities. This time of year they are looking for sweaters, coats and jackets, and heavier clothing, as the nights (even in Southern California) get quite cool.

November is also the ideal time to clean out our pantries, freezers and refrigerators. Take a look at what's in those spaces and see if some simple de-cluttering could help add some calm to your holiday season, long before Thanksgiving.

November is the best time of year to recognize others who have played such a significant role in our lives this past year or years. They probably don't need nor expect gifts of "things" from us, but rather would relish in "gifts of time" instead. Think about gifts of experiences, ones with you if that's appropriate or gifts of experiences they would enjoy themselves.

Have you ever kept a Gratitude Journal? This simple activity can have a profound impact on your emotional health. Right before going to bed or first thing in the morning, write down three things special about that day. You do not need a "fancy-dancy" expensive journal. This can be done in a steno notebook or other notebook you have at your home. Look around – I bet there's one there somewhere. I like to do this at night, reflecting on the finished day. For others they prefer first thing in the morning. The time of day is not as important as the habit and consistency. There's no perfect time to start, except now.

From now until the start of a new year many of us will be traveling. Throughout airports, train stations, and gas stops there will be many military members working to get home to their families or on to their next destination. Let's remember to thank them for their service when we see them or any other veterans.

"The willingness of America's veterans to sacrifice for our country has earned them our lasting gratitude."

– JEFF MILLER

"Be grateful for the home you have, knowing that at this moment all you have is all you need."

– SARAH BAN BREATHNACH

"Develop an attitude of gratitude, and give thanks for everything that happens to you, knowing that every step forward is a step toward achieving something bigger and better than your current situation."

– BRIAN TRACY

49. The Power of PLANNING

Wow-zee!

It's December already!

Where did the year go?

It sure flew by for me - maybe for you as well.

It's early December - time to remember to plan.

Quiet moments of planning can reduce stress, keep you calm, and help you stay in the moment.

I like to look at planning as Backward Mapping. Whether you want to plan holiday gift giving or entertaining, or a plan for successful living in the new year, now is the perfect time to put those dreams and ideas down in front of you.

Rather than having those thoughts rummage around in your head, turn to a blank sheet of paper in a notebook (no loose sheets of paper) or get a blank page on your computer and do a bit of dreaming.

Planning is the perfect antidote to stress. Without it we get into impulse buying, panic spending, or total inertia (I can't do _____ because I don't have enough time).

This week make a date with yourself for at least 60 minutes. With 168 hours in a week, surely you are worth giving yourself ONE of those hours. Get somewhere quiet - depending on your weather this time of year, outside in nature is always a great place for forward thinking.

Picture the end in mind, as Stephen Covey always used to talk about. If your business or personal life is going well, what does that look like to you? That's your end point.

Backward map from there.

For the really big planners out there, get a view from 30,000 feet - say three - five years out - and ask yourself, "What's my Vision for then?"

Maybe for you, you cannot possibly think like that because of chaos and conundrums facing you daily. So don't stress yourself by thinking that far into the future. See if you can come up with a plan for the day.

The night before, ask yourself one simple question, "If I want to count tomorrow as a success for me, the One Thing I need to do for the day is_____."

Too much gift giving and entertaining ahead for you this month? Ask yourself, "What can I eliminate here so that I can stay healthy through the season and enjoy it myself?"

That one question can provide you with the gift of sanity and that, my friends, is the ultimate gift to yourself.

Plan it and make it happen.

Wishing each of you a wonderful holiday season and the very best to you in the new year!

"Failure to plan is a plan to fail."
- BENJAMIN FRANKLIN

50. The Power of THE PRESENT

As the year winds down this month, the closure of December is always a great time for reflection. Did the year go as you had planned or were there some bumps and turns along the way? Life really is what happens to us while we're making other plans. I'm a planner and many of you are planners, while others just let each day unfold. Some of us approach life with awe and appreciation, and others with angst or possibly anger. The world is big enough for both the planners and the non-planners. For the planners it's tough though when things don't go "as planned."

Having a Plan "B" is something that's always on my mind. But for this month of December I am really going to focus on NOT planning, but rather being in the present, enjoying each gift of the day with its awesomeness, opportunities and yes, occasional bumps.

December can be one of the busiest months for many and one of the loneliest for others. For the remainder of the year let's heighten our senses; be aware and observe others as we go about our day. Check in with that quiet person at the coffee shop or the workroom. Raise our heads just a bit and see how they are really doing.

As we make purchases for gifts this holiday season think deeply first if that person needs ONE MORE THING or if he or she would relish a Gift of Time instead. Think about experiences and not things that take up space, need our attention and just add to our clutter and congestion.

Gifts of Time can come in many forms: sit still and think about the recipient.

Could they use an evening or afternoon away from their responsibilities? Would they enjoy a dinner and a movie with you? Might helping them complete a project be the best present you could give them this year?

Our presence with those we love and who love us is often the best present!

"If you are depressed, you are living in the past. If you are anxious, you are living in the future. If you are at peace, you are living in the present."

- LAO TZU

"Be present in all things and thankful for all things."

- MAYA ANGELOU

"Do not dwell in the past, do not dream of the future, concentrate the mind on the present moment."

- BUDDHA

"I know that the purpose of life is to understand and be in the present moment with the people you love. It's just that simple."

- JANE SEYMOUR

51. The Power of LEFTOVERS

For those of you with a Work Life (and who out there isn't working hard these days at something), think about your business/work goals you had set for the year back last January. Hopefully, those are written somewhere. Take a look at that list, and do an assessment.

Are you on track to finish the year strong with all the items you had planned on doing this year? If yes, great! Pat yourself on the back.

If not, review the list and see which item would give you the most sense of accomplishment and peace of mind if that ONE ITEM was moving forward in some way.

Maybe you had wanted to get your office organized, your files cleared out, your marketing plan updated, or obtain ten more clients. You might have wanted to get your home office paperwork in better shape so filing for taxes wasn't so... well, taxing!

Whatever it was, there is still time to make some progress. Block out some 60-90 minute blocks of focused time this week on your schedule and see what next steps you could take. Just keep it moving -- whatever the "it" is for you.

On the Home Front, often our attention turns to end of the year festivities. We can get consumed with lengthy to do lists, over-committed calendars and downright scary schedules. Let's step back from all that and take a couple of deep breaths.

It's not he or she with the longest To Do List who wins; it's really quite the contrary.

From a personal and home level, look over your list, and yes, I'm expecting you to have a checklist of sorts, instead of trying to keep all that running around in your great brain. Set a timer for twenty minutes of focused, uninterrupted time and thoroughly examine your end-of-the-year/holiday list.

Ask yourself:

Is everything on the list items you enjoy doing and get a great deal of pleasure from doing or are they tasks imposed by family, friends or others who just expect that year in and year out you will be the one to do the (fill in the blank here). Answers could be: party, turkey, elaborate four-day-dessert-making marathon, handmade gifts, specialty holiday cookie exchange, etc.

At the top of your list, cross out To Do and re-title it to Will Do. Look down the list and see if you can delegate any items to someone else. Put their initials next to the items. Look again and see if there are any you can delete - the world won't fall apart if these don't get done at all. Cross them out.

Now you should be left with a Will Do List that's reasonable.

*"A lot of things remain unfinished by the end of the day
and likewise remain incomplete by the end of life."*

- UNKNOWN

*"Go confidently in the direction of your dreams!
Live the life you've imagined."*

- HENRY DAVID THOREAU

52. The Power of REFLECTION

It's hard to believe another year is drawing to a close. The older one gets the faster the time goes. I hope the year has been good to you and that the dreams you had last January have come to fruition some time during the year. Hindsight, unfortunately, is always 20/20, and sometimes our best dreams and plans get interrupted by life's daily happenings and realities.

By the end of this year we should be a bit wiser, a little older, and a tad closer to our biggest dreams. Take time at the beginning of this month for some internal reflection. This can best be accomplished by writing some notes in a journal. Nothing fancy needed – even a steno notebook will do. Just you, pen and paper. Time to ask the hard questions: Did I accomplish my big goals for the year? If not, why not? Did these dreams even get a start? If so, congratulate yourself on that and reflect back as to why they didn't reach completion.

Now is the time to set up some systems for success going forward. What were the obstacles and the distractions? Were these preventable or not? What can you do now so that you are ready when the ball drops on New Year's Eve to kick-start the new year into high actionable steps of massive achievement? What things, behaviors or activities (or perhaps even people) are you able to let go of which impeded your progress to getting you to the life you imagine and deserve? Those are the things to write down now, just for your eyes.

"Without reflection, we go blindly on our way, creating more unintended consequences, and failing to achieve anything useful."

– Margaret J. Wheatley

"There are three methods to gaining wisdom. The first is reflection, which is the highest. The second is limitation, which is the easiest. The third is experience, which is the bitterest."

— CONFUCIUS

"Follow effective action with quiet reflection. From the quiet reflection will come even more effective action."

— PETER DRUCKER

Bonus - The Power of SELF-CARE

Just like on the airlines when they tell us if oxygen is needed, it's important to put our own mask on first, we need to work extra hard to stay healthy, hydrated and well-rested if we are going to be any good to others. This is the time of year where we need to let go of the martyr syndrome, along with the Martha Stewart syndrome. By that I mean we don't need to do it all and we certainly don't need to do it to a "Martha Stewart Home Standard."

We may have started the "Get Ready for the Holidays" Season at Halloween, thinking of making unique gifts for all the members of the family, baking special treats for all the people we appreciate who help make our world a little better and brighter, and cooking up a storm with the intricate recipes we viewed in the latest magazines.

Now is the time to get real - and get reasonable. If your calendar is clear in the next 10 days and you have the time and energy to do some or all of the above, hats off to you! Fabulous! Fantastic!

However, if you're like the rest of us, some extra projects may have crept into your schedule since October. Perhaps, the flu or a bad cold stopped by to knock you off your feet and calendar for a week or so. Maybe a home repair, like an emergency leak, raised its ugly head when you weren't looking. Perhaps problems at work crept into your calendar and consumed your calendar. As the expression goes, life happens while we're making other plans.

So forget about creating homemade holiday cards or homemade jam; let go of individually-designed by you Gingerbread Houses, worthy of an Architectural Digest award. This is the time of year to focus on what's really important: your religious celebrations, your close family members, and your gratitude for completing another year on life's journey.

*"Live in the moment with those you love and it
will remain forever through memories."*

-UNKNOWN

Final Thoughts

"All our dreams can come true if you have the courage to pursue them."
- Walt Disney

Thanks so much for taking the time to read this book. My hope for you is that it has spurred some action or stirred some dreams awake for you. Whether you are young or old, city or country, tall or short, my mission for you is that you take some steps toward what you want and deserve.

The chapters in this book are decidedly brief so that you can read several in a day or one in a day and ponder how it relates to you, wherever you are in your life right now.

Each of us is so unique with very specific skills and talents. Don't let your dreams die within you. You DO have the power within you to create the calm and focus you need to be more productive and transform yourself into the person you dream of becoming.

What are you waiting for?

"It's only too late if you never get started."

About the Author

Sue Crum, founder of 2020Vision4Success.com and ClearYourClutterCoach.com, has been helping people for many years to become more productive and live the life they imagine and deserve.

Sue is a #1 International Best-selling Author, Motivational Speaker, and Certified High Performance Coach. Sue has received specialized training from Jack Canfield, co-creator of the #1 Best-selling series Chicken Soup for the Soul™, author of "The Success Principles," and star of the hit movie, "The Secret." As a Certified Canfield Methodology Trainer and Certified Success Principles Trainer, Sue loves to serve on Jack's Assisting Team during his multi-day and one-day specialized presentations of The Success Principles.

Before her work helping others to better productivity and focus, Sue served in multiple school districts in the following leadership positions: acting superintendent, assistant superintendent, principal - three schools (middle and elementary) and assistant principal - junior high.

Sue holds a doctorate degree in organizational leadership from the University of Southern California, a master's degree from California State University, Los Angeles, and a bachelor's degree from Bradley University, Peoria, Illinois.

After 21 winters in Illinois, Sue decided there might be better weather somewhere else! Upon graduating from Bradley, she bought her first car, a red convertible at age 21, thanked her parents for raising her and drove to Southern California, where, ironically, she became a black diamond downhill skier with an annual season ski pass!

When Sue is not speaking on productivity, focus and taking action or coaching others virtually, Sue can be found downhill skiing in the winter or doing stand-up paddle boarding the rest of the year. She lives at the beach in San Diego County with her handsome and helpful husband and their neurotic dog from rescue.

Coaching

Want to upgrade your life to the one you've imagined and deserve?

Let Sue work with you in one of her coaching programs and help you take back your power.

Schedule a Breakthrough Call with Sue to discuss your specific needs. Go to

<u>2020Vision4Success.com/apply</u>

In Need of a Speaker for Your Next Event?

Sue Crum is an experienced, motivational speaker who would love to present to your association, business or group.

Sue's mission is to inspire and empower others to get on with the life they imagine and deserve through improved focus, better productivity and targeted action.

Download her speaking brochure at:

<u>SueCrum.com/meeting-planners</u>

Contact her at sue@suecrum.com or 760.479.6680 to discuss your specific needs.

Want MORE Inspiration?

MY TOP TEN FAVORITE BOOKS FOR THE POWER OF YOU

Babauta, Leo
> Focus

Canfield, Jack
> The Success Principles: How to Get From Where You Are to Where You Want to Be

Cohen, Darlene
> The One Who Is Not Busy

Covey, Stephen
> The Seven Habits of Highly Effective People

Crum, Sue
> Clear Your Clutter: 50 Ways to Organize Your Life, Home or Business So You Can Become More Calm, Focused & Happy

Gordon, Britton & Page
> One Word That Will Change Your Life

Hadamuscin, John
> Simple Pleasures: 101 Thoughts and Recipes for Savoring the Little Things in Life

Hill, Napoleon
> Think and Grow Rich

McRaven, Admiral William H.
> Make Your Bed: Little Things That Can Change Your Life and Maybe the World

Rimes, Shonda
> Year of Yes

Shinoff, Marci
> Happy for No Reason

Tracy, Brian
> Eat That Frog
> No Excuses

CPSIA information can be obtained
at www.ICGtesting.com
Printed in the USA
FSHW020105100219
55541FS